Prayer Book
of the Early Christians

Prayer Book
of the Early Christians

Translated and Edited by
JOHN A. MCGUCKIN

PARACLETE PRESS
BREWSTER, MASSACHUSETTS

Prayer Book of the Early Christians

2011   First Printing

Copyright © 2011 by John A. McGuckin

ISBN: 978-1-55725-702-4

Scriptures, other than the Psalms, are the author's own paraphrases using the *Revised Standard Version of the Bible* or the original Greek.

The Psalm texts are the author's own emendations of the Grail Psalter (England), © 1963, 1986 The Grail. All rights reserved.

Library of Congress Cataloging-in-Publication Data

Prayer book of the early Christians / translated and edited by John A. McGuckin.
     p. cm.
  Includes bibliographical references.
  ISBN 978–1–55725–702–4 (hard cover)
  1. Prayers. I. McGuckin, John Anthony.
  BV245.P785 2011
  242.8—dc23

                                           2011037126

10 9 8 7 6 5 4 3 2 1

Published by Paraclete Press
Brewster, Massachusetts
www.paracletepress.com
Printed in the United States of America

CONTENTS

A GUIDE AND INTRODUCTION
FOR THE USE OF THIS BOOK OF PRAYER

This book has been compiled mainly for the use of ordinary Christians in domestic circumstances. It is heavily based upon the ritual books of the Eastern Orthodox Church, to which I myself belong, but represents also the prayers of many worldwide Christians from ancient times: the Syrians of Antioch (where the name "Christian" was first used); the Copts and Ethiopians of Africa who were evangelized in apostolic times; the prayers and devotions of Roman, Greek, Russian, Armenian, and other Christian churches, as they have been recorded by the great saints down the ages. These are prayers that have been tried and proved.

They have more than withstood the test of time and are filled with the grace of the saints who first used them and passed them down to us. For this book, I have made new versions of all these ancient sources, trying to lift them up anew, like treasures from antiquity as it were, and polish them so as to gleam in modern, elegant English. All the time I have been moved to render the texts with an eye to poetically workable lines and stanzas. Almost all of these prayers were originally composed in the church with a lively ear for their assonance—their artistic communal ability to express the heart's intentions before God by the grace of the artistry of language. This prayer book tries its hardest to be poetic without appearing to be such; to be elegant while at the same time modern; to be informal without being colloquial.

Many of the suggested services of domestic prayer can be said entirely by one person leading all the prayers. At certain times (such

as prayers on the occasion of the death of a loved one), it is better
to have one person who is able to lead the prayers in a quiet and
calm voice, than it is to pass round the various parts, especially if
many people present are incapable (because of grief for example) of
really taking a leading role. At other times, a group of people can
pass round the task of saying various parts. Each time the Psalms are
written down in this book they are done so in a way that normally
divides them up into "verses" of two lines. This is an easy way for
half of a group (one side of a room, for example) to say one verse, and
another side to make the (antiphonal) response. The Psalms version
that has been generally used (with some small amendments) is the
delightful "Grail" version, which I have loved since it first appeared
in 1963 from that group of learned Catholic scholars and ascetics
who first made it, emphasizing the poetic nature of the Psalms, for
their own sung daily worship. The entire Grail Psalter is available
for open access download on the Internet (typing "Grail Psalms" in
Google will direct you to the site).

YOUR BASIC PRAYER KIT

When Christians pray, from time immemorial they have lit candles.
The candle is a sign of the fire of the Holy Spirit. Their cheerful
radiance (especially if at the time of prayer one dims the lights a
little) becomes a little sacrament of the resurrection grace of Christ.
The flame also serves to remind us of how pure and heartfelt our
prayer is meant to be, even if, at times, we are praying in a doldrum
and may hardly feel any grace at all. The candle reminds us that
Christ and his Holy Spirit pray in and through us, unfailingly. They
see the heart's intent and always draw close in time of prayer. Their
prayer (in us, through us, over us) is never dim, always luminous.
Each home can have a candle present, always ready at time of prayer.

In addition to a candle, one might also wish to have a "basic prayer kit" of a cross (wooden or metal) and an icon of Christ, or the Virgin Mother with Christ.

Throughout this book, there appears a small cross + at the beginning of some of the lines, as well as at the start and completion of prayers. This is the mark where all present should make the sign of the cross over themselves.[1] The name of the Father, Son, and Spirit is one name, the living name of the one God who is Trinity. This great and ancient prayer can be made anywhere as a sign of blessing over us or others, as a call for God's protection and help. It is the prayer that seals all others. The ancient prophets throughout the Holy Scriptures taught that where the Name of God is, there is the presence of God too, and his active power. Where the cross is, no evil or harm can endure.

Most Orthodox homes have set aside a little corner of the house (often in the main room in the corner looking toward the east) that they call the "Beautiful Corner," where one finds the family icons and the cross and the prayer books, and where a believer might stand at morning and night to say the prayers. It does not have to be in the eastern corner if this is not convenient. It is often better to be somewhere out of the way and quiet. In ancient times, the icons were often the most beautiful things a family possessed, and even the children were drawn to look at them: beauty attracting beauty. It is, after all, an old saying that gives us a good concept for Christian training of the young that "the things you love as a child you will love all your life long." And what better than to have instilled even from childhood a heartfelt desire for prayer, a love of the beautiful so that prayer is not a chore or a burdensome task, but something that one can look forward to each day. Even when we may be in a time of dryness or despondency, if our prayer corner is bright, beautiful, radiant with candle flame and the sweet smell of incense, it can raise up our hearts, reminding us of the beauty of God, such that turning to prayer can serve as a radiant oasis even in a gloomy desert of a day.

A NOTE ON THE USE OF THE PSALMS

It is the ancient custom of the Eastern and Western churches, Orthodox and Catholic, to number the Psalms liturgically in the way they are listed in the Greek (Septuagint or LXX) Bible, which the earliest Christians always used. Only after the time of the Reformation in the late Renaissance did the Protestant world change this custom to start using the Psalms as they are listed in the Hebraic Bible. The present prayer book refers to the psalms in Orthodox and Catholic custom, as they are referenced liturgically; in other words, in the Septuagintal numbering. This is slightly different from the Bibles many readers may have in their homes that follow the Protestant system of numbering. In most cases the ancient liturgical reference is going to be one psalm behind. If one has a Protestant Bible, the following chart will give the equivalent reading. All other biblical passages are the same in all editions of Scripture:

Liturgical/Septuagintal Psalm Numbers As used in this book.	*Hebraic/Protestant System*
1–8	1–8
9	9–10
10–112	11–113
113	114–15
114–15	116
116–45	117–46
146–47	147
148–150	148–50

With this in mind, let me commend the book of Psalms to the reader as a major resource—one of those things to be held alongside a cross and a candle and an icon as a "basic kit for serious prayer" in any Christian house.

As well as a cross, a candle, and so on, one needs to have a copy of the Gospels. The Gospels and the book of Psalms are the two basic "sacred texts" from which our prayer kit is constructed.

THE ART OF PRAYER

One's basic prayer kit is gathered now: a special corner or part of the house set aside as a domestic altar containing an icon, a cross, a book of prayers, a copy of the Psalms, and the book of the Gospels (which ought to be bound or covered with especially "joyous" bindings or coverings; in ancient times they used gold and silver and enamels, and we might have to make do with festive paper, but the point still remains). One has an icon lamp or a candle here too. At the time of prayer in morning or evening, light a candle when you start prayer. In Orthodox homes, the faithful usually have a small home censer (Orthodox sites on the Internet offer them for sale) and a small amount of charcoal with a few grains of incense on top, for praying (especially in the evening): "Let my prayer arise like incense in your sight, O Lord." If one wishes to offer incense, the suitable places are marked in the text for morning and evening. Offering incense to God was a basic ritual of the ancient temple in Jerusalem and has remained integral to most Catholic and all Orthodox rituals. In the Eastern churches, the ordinary faithful laity also offer incense at home during their prayers—a lively reminder of their priestly status and dignity as baptized and chrismated servants of God. Whenever we pray, we stand as cosmic priests of Christ at the heart of the grace of salvation, which is the ongoing divine process of the metamorphosing of materiality into the light of glory.

Always be glad to come to pray. Never allow it to become a "chore." When one starts to have a regular prayer life, what first seemed like the most pleasant part of the whole day—a quiet time given over to God—will soon enough become a time when one would rather dig the garden or climb on the roof (anything at all!) in order to avoid prayer. This is a normal reaction. The correct way to meet this *acedie* (spiritual dryness) is to not be bothered by it and to not give it any real significance.

It does not really matter whether we feel fervent or dry as a bone. It does not really matter whether we feel God's presence breathing on our face or feel as if he is locked up behind a bronze heaven, never showing a sign of his presence. What matters is how he sees us. We do not need to "feel" his presence at every turn, when we know, by faith, that he is more present to us, at every moment of our life, than we are present to ourselves or our most beloved family. And if at morning and night we present ourselves before God and sing his praise, we have (no question about it) stood in the presence of Christ, prayed along with Christ our High Priest in the pure presence of the Holy Spirit of God, and offered our prayer like incense in the sight of the Father.

In being faithful day after day, we establish a habit, like that of healthy eating or good exercise, and our lives are changed dramatically at the core. We stand in the presence of the craftsmen and women of the Spirit of God who have gone before us.

Most of the prayers here are designed to be fairly short, not demanding too much time. If one wants to extend them, it is easy enough to weave in more psalms or more readings from the Gospel, or to begin the Jesus Prayer, about which there is a short concluding note at the end of this book—a brief word about a mystical subject of such profundity it properly escapes speech. Also, perhaps, one might find it very helpful to find a book of the writings of the ancient saints on prayer (there are so many in the ancient Christian tradition, and so many modern spiritual classics). One can use these writings in the manner of *lectio divina*—reading a few paragraphs, leaving the book aside, mulling over what the author has said about the Christ life and how is it like that in our own Christ life—always with a view to dialogue with the presence of the Christ here and now.[2]

By "short" and "long," in our modern domestic circumstances, I am talking of something relative. Twenty minutes seems a long time for a pressed twenty-first-century dweller. Longer than that, we may want to set a small timer to mark our time of praying, for those who swim the ocean of prayer find that time starts shrinking. The monks of Athos even today sometimes spend thirteen hours a day in prayer. They are, undoubtedly, something of an exception!

God sees the willing soul who sets out on a journey of prayer. He never fails to bless the generosity of such a soul and confirm the priestly role of the one who prays—even if at the end of the time of prayer one feels very deeply a "could-have-done-better" sensation. That does not matter. He sees our intent more than he sees our accomplishments: and he has pity on us because of it and blesses us anyway in his immense love for our race.

May God bless you as you pick up this book, strengthen you as you set off on the road of prayer using it, and bring you speedily to that place at the end of the road where the church of God is merrily assembled in the light of the Father's mansions—entertaining the Head of our vast extended family and being entertained by him in such wondrous company.

Fr. John A. McGuckin
Priest of the Romanian Orthodox Church
Feast of St. Basil the Great
New York, January 1, 2011

Prayer Book
of the Early Christians

PART 1

Ritual Offices of Prayer for the Whole Day

The services that constitute the first part of this book of prayers are (fundamentally) based upon the cycle of daily prayers ("Offices" of the early church) as they appear in the Eastern Christian Church's Book of Hours. The shorter ones are more or less as they are commonly used today in Orthodox monasteries across the world. The longer ones, especially Vespers and Matins, have been simplified here from the very complex forms they have evolved into across many centuries, forms that today would require a skilled cantor using several different books of daily "propers" to complete them accurately. This present format scales them all down to make a usable and approachable "Ritual of Offices" for use in a domestic situation, even a daily use, for a single person or for small groups of family or friends praying the Offices together.

The Offices of the Church (or "Hours") are its most ancient structured form of prayer after the Holy Eucharist. The great sacrament of the Eucharist was always regarded as being in no time or place other than the *eschaton*: the eighth day of new creation, outside the seven days of this age. On the one hand, the Eucharist is the timeless celebration—everywhere and nowhere—for it is also celebrated in heaven as we embark upon it on earth, since angels gather among us to share it. The Eucharist, then, does not mark out time: it anticipates the ending of time in the here and now. It is the ancient sacrifice of the Lord made always new, ever-present. It only has a present tense, a *Parousia*, as the New Testament calls it. The Hours, on the other hand, are exactly the "measuring out" of the times that intervene in the pilgrimage of the church between the beginning of our journey, after Pentecost, and our completion, when we enter into the kingdom of the Lord. The Hours are the heartbeat of the church's existence on earth. They mark the day into rhythms of prayer and thanksgiving. They join us as cocelebrants with the angels and saints of all times, and catch us up, out of the time-bound, into the eternal.

For centuries the Daily Offices have been largely the preserve of the clergy. Monks and nuns still revolve their days around these offices. The priests of the church used to recite these prayers as basic elements of their daily prayers. In recent times, there has been a solid liturgical revival in the church of both East and West, reclaiming these prayers as the basic ritual of worship for all the church—reclaiming them for the laity. If one ever gets the chance to pray these offices formally in church, together with monastics and clergy, it will be a blessing. Before this happens once more as a regular part of "ecclesial" experience for most, the opportunity to get to know them in private prayer at home is a great blessing too.

An Office of Evening Prayers at Dusk
VESPERS
(A Simple Rite of Lucernarium)

*The earliest known structured form of Vespers in the church dates as far back
as Hippolytus of Rome and was widely practiced by the early fourth century.
It was not simply a monastic service but was observed also in the homes of all
the faithful. It was always marked by a simple rhythm of the natural world,
taking place every evening as the daylight started to dim with the onset of dusk.
The chief rituals involved were the lighting of the domestic lamps (or the lamps
in the church before the icons) while singing the ancient hymn "O Gladsome
Light" and the offering of incense to God "as an evening sacrifice of praise"
while reciting the core text of Psalms 103 and 142.*

*The onset of evening still can mark for us a song of hope in the face of
the encroaching darkness and (as the Church, following the ancient Temple
rituals, believed) the beginning of a new day—simultaneously a time for
endings and for new hopes. If one has a domestic incense burner, one can
safely offer incense to the glory of God as the ancient priests used to do in the
Jerusalem temple at the time of evening prayers. One may also light a small
lamp (a tea light in a safety glass standing before an icon is customary among
the Orthodox). The offering of incense and the lighting of the lamps of evening
were basic parts of the ritual and still are memorable aspects of consecrating
the "hours" to God.*

OPENING PRAYER OF BLESSING

+ Blessed is our God. Always now and ever and
to the ages of ages. Amen.

*The Orthodox usually say "Through the prayers of our holy Fathers and
Mothers, Lord Jesus Christ our God, have mercy on us and save us."
This prayer, known as the "Seal," is used to begin all common prayer services.*

TRISAGION PRAYERS

(The word Trisagion *comes from the Greek for "Thrice Holy"—
one of the key prayers in the sequence.)*

O Heavenly King, the Paraclete, the Spirit of Truth, who are present everywhere, filling all things, Treasury of Good and Giver of Life, come and dwell in us, cleanse us of every stain, and save our souls, O Good One.

+ Holy God, Holy Mighty, Holy Immortal, have mercy on us.
  (three times)
+ Glory to the Father, and to the Son, and to the Holy Spirit.
  Now and ever and to the ages of ages. Amen.

All-Holy Trinity, have mercy on us. Lord, forgive us our sins. Master, pardon our transgressions. Holy One, visit and heal our infirmities for your name's sake.

Lord have mercy   Lord have mercy   Lord have mercy

+ Glory to the Father, and to the Son, and to the Holy Spirit.
  Now and ever and to the ages of ages. Amen.

Our Father in heaven, hallowed be your name. Your kingdom come. Your will be done, on earth as it is in heaven. Give us this day our daily bread, and forgive us our trespasses as we forgive those who trespass against us, and do not lead us into temptation, but deliver us from the evil one. (For Yours is the kingdom and the power and the glory, of the Father, and of the Son, and of the Holy Spirit, now and ever and to the ages of ages.) + Amen.

Lord have mercy   Lord have mercy   *(six times)*

+ Glory to the Father, and to the Son, and to the Holy Spirit.
  Now and ever and to the ages of ages. Amen.

INVITATORY PRAYER

+ Come let us worship and bow down before God our King.
  (bowing low each time)
+ Come let us worship and bow down before Christ, our King and God.
+ Come let us worship and bow down before Christ himself,
  our King and our God.

Psalm 103
*(The psalms may be recited in alternating
double lines by more than one person.)*

Bless the Lord, my soul!
Lord God, how great you are,

Clothed in majesty and glory,
Wrapped in light as in a robe!

You stretch out the heavens like a tent.
Above the rains you build your dwelling.

You make the clouds your chariot,
You walk on the wings of the wind,

You make the winds your messengers
And flashing fire your servants.

You founded the earth on its base,
To stand firm from age to age.

You wrapped it with the ocean like a cloak:
The waters stood higher than the mountains.

At your threat they took to flight;
At the voice of your thunder they fled.

They rose over the mountains
And flowed down to the place which you had appointed.

You set limits they might not pass
Lest they return to cover the earth.

You make springs gush forth in the valleys;
They flow in between the hills.

They give drink to all the beasts of the field;
The wild asses quench their thirst.

On their banks dwell the birds of heaven;
From the branches they sing their song.

From your dwelling you water the hills;
Earth drinks its fill of your gift.

You make the grass grow for the cattle
And plants to serve our needs

That we may bring forth bread from the earth
And wine to cheer the heart;

Oil, to make the face shine
And bread to strengthen the heart.

The trees of the Lord drink their fill,
The cedars he planted on Lebanon;

There the birds build their nests;
On the treetop the stork has her home.

The goats find a home on the mountains,
And rabbits hide in the rocks.

You made the moon to mark the months;
The sun knows the time for its setting.

When you spread the darkness it is night
And all the beasts of the forest creep forth.

Young lions roar for their prey,
And ask their food from God.

At the rising of the sun they steal away
And go to rest in their dens.

We go forth to our work,
To labor till evening falls.

How many are your works, O Lord!
In wisdom you have made them all.

The earth is full of your riches.
There is the sea, vast and wide,

With its moving swarms past counting,
Living things great and small.

The ships are moving there
And the monsters you made to play with.

All of these look to you,
To give them their food in due season.

You give it, they gather it up:
You open your hand, they have their fill.

You hide your face, they are dismayed;
You take back your spirit, they die,
Returning to the dust from which they came.

You send forth your spirit, they are created;
And you renew the face of the earth.

May the glory of the Lord last forever!
May the Lord rejoice in his works!

He looks on the earth and it trembles;
The mountains send forth smoke at his touch.

I will sing to the Lord all my life,
Make music to my God while I live.

May my thoughts be pleasing to him.
I find my joy in the Lord.

Let sinners vanish from the earth
And the wicked exist no more.

Bless the Lord, my soul.

> \+ Glory to the Father, and to the Son, and to the Holy Spirit.
> Now and ever and to the ages of ages. Amen.
>
> Alleluia, Alleluia, Alleluia. Glory to you, O God. *(three times)*

PRAYER OF EVENTIDE

In the evening and in the morning and at noonday we praise you, we bless you, we give you thanks, and we pray to you, Master of All, Lord who loves humankind. Direct our prayer as incense before you, and do not incline our hearts to words or deeds of evil, but deliver us from all who seek after our souls. Lord, our eyes have looked to you. In you have we hoped. Do not put us to shame, our God,

> \+ For to you are due all glory, honor, and worship:
> Now and ever and to the ages of ages. Amen.

Psalm 140

Incense may be offered here before the icons or the cross.

Lord, I have cried to you, hear me, O Lord!
Lord, I have cried to you, hear me, O Lord!
Attend to the voice of my prayer,
Hear me when I call to you.
Let my prayer come before you like incense;
The raising of my hands like an evening oblation.

PRAYER OVER THE INCENSE
(said quietly)

+ Incense we offer you, O Christ our God. Accept it at your heavenly throne, and send down upon us, in return, the grace of your Holy Spirit.

THEOTOKION—HYMN TO THE VIRGIN

Let us sing the praises of the Virgin Mary, the Gate of Heaven, and glory of the world. Though born of mortal kind, she bore the Lord of all. She is the song of the Bodiless Powers, the adornment of all the faithful. She has been revealed as a Heaven, a Temple of the Deity. Tearing down the dividing wall of enmity, she ushered in peace and opened out the kingdom. Holding fast to her, the Anchor of our faith, we shall have a strong Defender, the Very Lord who was born of her. Take courage, then, people of God, and be of good heart, for he, the All-Powerful, will cast down all our foes.

LIGHTING THE LAMP OF EVENING

A lamp or candle should be lighted now before the icons or the cross. If the incense is still burning, the censer is lifted up three times crosswise at the words "Father, Son, and Holy Spirit" as an act of worship to the Divine Trinity

O Jesus Christ, the Gladdening Light
Of the Immortal Father's holy glory;
The Heavenly, Holy, Blessed One;
As the sun declines, we see the light of evening,
And sing our hymn to God: + the Father, Son, and Holy Spirit.
Worthy are you, O Son of God, through each and every moment,
That joyful songs should hymn you.
You are the Giver of our Life,
And so the world gives glory.

LITANY OF INTERCESSION

In peace let us pray to the Lord.	Lord have mercy
For the church of God across the face of the earth	Lord have mercy
For all who live faithfully, seeking Christ's will	Lord have mercy
For the suffering and the homeless	Lord have mercy
For captives and their salvation	Lord have mercy
For the oppressed and their deliverance	Lord have mercy
For the sick and the despairing	Lord have mercy
For those who have suffered loss or great sorrow	Lord have mercy
For our strengthening in joy and hope	Lord have mercy
For . . . *(the names and causes we wish to pray for)*	Lord have mercy
For all of us who call on you from our hearts	Lord have mercy
	Lord have mercy
	Lord have mercy

FINAL EVENING PRAYER

O God, you are great and wonderful; you govern all things in unspeakable goodness and bountiful providence. You have given us earthly benefits and even granted us a pledge of the promised kingdom by already favoring us with its graces. You have preserved us from all evil works during that part of the day which has now passed; grant now that we may complete the remainder of it blamelessly in the face of your holy glory, and hymn you, the only Good One, our God who loves mankind. For you are our God, + and to you we ascribe glory, to the Father, and to the Son, and to the Holy Spirit, now and ever and to the ages of ages. Amen.

CONCLUDING PRAYER OF BLESSING

+ May God have compassion on us and bless us;
    May he show the light of his countenance to us, and be merciful
    to us. Amen.

*(Or the "Seal": Through the prayers of our holy Fathers and Mothers, Lord
    Jesus Christ our God, have mercy on us and save us.)*

Other Ancient Prayers for Evening Time

These were the ancient "lychnapsia" (lamp lighting) prayers, once said by the priest silently, but so rich that they might be usefully said aloud, in whole or in part, by anyone praying this ritual—by a single person or a group who says them quietly while others simultaneously recite the psalms. They are beautiful general and supplemental evening prayers for any Christian to use.

1. O Lord, compassionate and merciful, long-suffering and plentiful in mercy, attend to the voice of our prayer. Work upon us a sign for the good. Lead us in your way, that we may walk in the truth. Gladden our hearts that we may honor your holy name. For you are great and work wonders. You alone are God, and among all the powers there is none like you, our Lord, who is mighty in mercy, gracious in strength, always ready to aid and to comfort and save those who put their trust in your holy name. + And to you are due all glory, honor, and worship. Now and ever and to the ages of ages. Amen.

2. O Lord, do not rebuke us in your wrath, and do not chastise us in your anger, but always deal with us in your accustomed mercifulness, O Physician and Healer of our souls. Guide us to the harbor of your will. Enlighten the eyes of our hearts in the knowledge of your truth, and grant that what remains of this day, and indeed our whole life, may be peaceful and sinless. We ask this through the intercessions of the Holy Mother of God and of all the saints: for yours is the might, and yours is the kingdom and the power and the glory, + of the Father, and of the Son, and of the Holy Spirit, now and ever and to the ages of ages. Amen.

3. O Lord our God, remember us sinners, your unprofitable servants, when we call upon your holy name, and do not take from us the expectation of your mercy, but instead, Lord, grant all our requests that are useful to salvation, and grant that we may love and honor you with all our hearts, and do your will in all things; for you are a good God who loves mankind. And to you we ascribe glory, + to the Father, and to the Son, and to the Holy Spirit, now and ever and to the ages of ages. Amen.

4. You who are celebrated by the never-silent hymns and unceasing doxologies of the Holy Powers: fill our mouths with your praise that we may magnify your holy name. And give to us a share and inheritance alongside all who truly honor you and keep your commandments, through the intercessions of the Holy Mother of God and of all your saints, for to you are due all glory, honor, and worship, + to the Father, and to the Son, and to the Holy Spirit, now and ever and to the ages of ages. Amen.

5. Lord, O Lord, who hold all things in the spotless hollow of your hand, and who are long-suffering to us all, yet grieved at our wickedness: remember your compassions and your mercy. Look down on us in your goodness, and grant that through the remainder of this day we may avoid the varied subtle snares of the evil one, by your grace. Guard our life from all dangers + through the grace of your All-Holy Spirit, and through the philanthropic mercy and love of your Only Begotten Son, with whom you are blessed always, now and ever and to the ages of ages. Amen.

6. O God, who are great and wonderful, who govern all things in unspeakable goodness and generous providence, who have given us earthly benefits and even granted us a pledge of the promised kingdom by already favoring us with its benefits, you who have preserved us from all evil inclinations during that part of the day which is now past, grant now that we may complete the remainder of it blameless in the sight of your holy glory, and hymn you, the only Good One, our God who loves mankind. For you are our God, and to you we ascribe glory, + to the Father, and to the Son, and to the Holy Spirit, now and ever and to the ages of ages. Amen.

7. O Great and Most High God, who alone have immortality and dwell in inaccessible light; you who have made all creation in wisdom and have divided the light from the darkness and appointed the sun to rule the day, the moon and the stars to rule the night; you who have granted us sinners even at this present hour to come before you with confession, to offer you our evening praise: may you yourself, Philanthropic Lord, direct our prayer as incense before you, and accept it as an odor of sweet fragrance. Grant that we may pass this present evening and the coming night in peace. Put on us the armor of light. Deliver us from the terror of the night, and from everything that walks in darkness, and grant that our sleep, which you have appointed for the repose of our weakness, may be free from every fantasy of the devil. And Master, who give us every good thing, may we be moved to penitence even upon our beds and call to mind your name in the night, so that enlightened by meditating on your commandments we may rise up in gladness of soul to glorify your goodness, presenting renewed prayers and petitions to your tenderness of heart, both on account of our own failings and those of all your people; so that through the intercessions of the Holy Mother of God you might look

down on them all with mercy. For you are a good God, who loves mankind, and to you we ascribe glory, + to the Father, and to the Son, and to the Holy Spirit, now and ever and to the ages of ages. Amen.

An Office of Night Prayers
COMPLINE

Night Prayer, or Compline, is the service traditionally said immediately before retiring to sleep. It is a gentle service reminding the believer of the "closure" that sleep brings to a day (a symbol, theologically speaking, of death and the trust in God that this requires of us). It ought to be recited calmly, peacefully, with an emphasis on the laying of our whole life, all its aspirations and fears, into the hands of the Living God, who is also the profoundly Loving God, Father of our souls and bodies.

OPENING PRAYER OF BLESSING

+ Blessed is our God. Always now and ever and to the ages of ages. Amen.

Or the "Seal": Through the prayers of our holy Fathers and Mothers, Lord Jesus Christ our God, have mercy on us and save us. Amen.

Glory to you, our God, glory to you.

TRISAGION PRAYERS
(repeat from pages 8–9)

INVITATORY PRAYER

+ Come let us worship and bow down before God our King.
  (bowing low each time)
+ Come let us worship and bow down before Christ, our King and God.
+ Come let us worship and bow down before Christ himself, our King and our God.

Psalm 50[3]

Have mercy on me, God, in your kindness.
In your compassion blot out my offense.

Wash me more and more from my guilt,
And cleanse me from my sin.

My offenses truly I know them;
My sin is always before me

Against you, you alone, have I sinned;
What is evil in your sight I have done.

That you may be justified when you give sentence
And be without reproach when you judge,

O see, in guilt I was born,
A sinner was I conceived.

Indeed you love truth in the heart;
Then in the secret of my heart teach me wisdom.

Purify me, then I shall be clean;
Wash me, I shall be whiter than snow.

Make me hear rejoicing and gladness,
That the bones you have crushed may thrill.

From my sins turn away your face
And blot out all my guilt.

A pure heart create for me, O God,
Put a steadfast spirit within me.

Do not cast me away from your presence,
Nor deprive me of your holy spirit.

Give me again the joy of your help;
With a spirit of fervor sustain me,

That I may teach transgressors your ways
And sinners may return to you.

O rescue me, God, my helper,
And my tongue shall ring out your goodness.

O Lord, open my lips
And my mouth shall declare your praise.

For in sacrifice you take no delight,
Burnt offering from me you would refuse,

My sacrifice, a contrite spirit,
A humbled, contrite heart you will not spurn.

In your goodness, show favor to Zion:
Rebuild the walls of Jerusalem.

Then you will be pleased with lawful sacrifice,
(Burnt offerings wholly consumed),
Then you will be offered young bulls on your altar.

Psalm 69

O God, make haste to my rescue,
Lord, come to my aid!

O let there be shame and confusion
On those who seek my life.

Let them turn back in confusion,
Who delight in my harm,

Let them retreat, covered with shame,
Who jeer at my lot.

Let there be rejoicing and gladness
For all who seek you.

Let them say for ever: "God is great,"
Who love your saving help.

As for me, wretched and poor,
Come to me, O God.

You are my rescuer, my help,
O Lord, do not delay.

Psalm 142

Lord, listen to my prayer: turn your ear to my appeal.
You are faithful, you are just; give answer.

Do not call your servant to judgment
For no one is just in your sight.

The enemy pursues my soul;
He has crushed my life to the ground;

He has made me dwell in darkness
Like the dead, long forgotten.

Therefore my spirit fails;
My heart is numb within me.

I remember the days that are past:
I ponder all your works.

I muse on what your hand has wrought
And to you I stretch out my hands.
Like a parched land my soul thirsts for you.

Lord, make haste and answer;
For my spirit fails within me.

Do not hide your face
Lest I become like those in the grave.

In the morning let me know your love
For I put my trust in you.

Make me know the way I should walk:
To you I lift up my soul.

Rescue me, Lord, from my enemies;
I have fled to you for refuge.

Teach me to do your will
For you, O Lord, are my God.

Let your good spirit guide me
In ways that are level and smooth.

For your name's sake, Lord, save my life;
In your justice save my soul from distress.

In your love make an end of my foes;
Destroy all those who oppress me
For I am your servant, O Lord.

Psalm 90

One who dwells in the shelter of the Most High
And abides in the shade of the Almighty

Says to the Lord: "My refuge,
My stronghold, my God in whom I trust!"

It is he who will free you from the snare of the fowler
Who seeks to destroy you;

He will conceal you with his pinions
And under his wings you will find refuge.

You will not fear the terror of the night
Nor the arrow that flies by day,

Nor the plague that prowls in the darkness,
Nor the scourge that lays waste at noon.

A thousand may fall at your side,
Ten thousand fall at your right,

You, it will never approach;
His faithfulness is buckler and shield.

Your eyes have only to look
To see how the wicked are repaid,

You who have said: "Lord, my refuge!"
And have made the Most High your dwelling.

Upon you no evil shall fall,
No plague approach where you dwell.

For you has he commanded his angels,
To keep you in all your ways.

They shall bear you upon their hands
Lest you strike your foot against a stone.

On the lion and the viper you will tread
And trample the young lion and the dragon.

One who clings to me in love, I will set free:
Protect the one who knows my name.

Call out and I shall answer: I am with you.
I will save you in distress and give you glory.

With length of life I will content you.
I shall let you see my saving power.

+ Glory to the Father, and to the Son, and to the Holy Spirit.
Now and ever and to the ages of ages. Amen.

+ Alleluia, Alleluia, Alleluia, glory to you, O God. *(three times)*

THE DOXOLOGY

Glory to God in the highest and on earth peace, and good will among all.
We praise you, we bless you, we worship you,
We glorify you, and we give thanks to you for your great glory:
Lord, the heavenly King, God the Father Almighty,
Lord, the Only Begotten Son, Jesus Christ, and the Holy Spirit.

Lord God, Lamb of God, Son of the Father, who take away the sin
of the world,
Have mercy on us, you who take away the sin of the world.
Receive our prayer, you who sit at the right hand of the Father, and
have mercy on us;
For you alone are holy, you alone are Lord, Jesus Christ, to the glory
of God the Father.

Each day I will bless you and praise your name forever,
and to the ages.
Lord, you have been our refuge from one generation to the next.
O Lord have mercy on me; heal my soul, for I have sinned against
you.
Lord, I have fled to you for refuge; teach me to do your will,
for you are my God.

In you is the fountain of life. In your light we shall see light.

Continue your mercy to those who know you.

Grant, Lord, to keep us this night without sin.

Blessed are you, O Lord, the God of generations.

Praised and glorified is your name, to the ages. Amen.

Let your mercy rest upon us, Lord, as we have placed our hope in you.

Blessed are you, Lord; teach me your statutes.

Blessed are you, Master; make me understand your statutes.

Blessed are you, Holy One; illuminate me by your statutes.

Lord, your mercy lasts forever: do not despise the work of your hands.

To you praise is fitting; to you song is fitting; to you glory is fitting:

+ To the Father, and to the Son, and to the Holy Spirit.

Now and ever and to the ages of ages. Amen.

THEOTOKION—SONG TO THE VIRGIN

It is truly fitting to call you blessed, Theotokos, the all-blessed and all-immaculate Mother of our God. More honorable than the Cherubim and incomparably more glorious than the Seraphim, for as a virgin you gave birth to God the Word. Truly the Mother of God, we magnify you.

TRISAGION PRAYERS
(repeat from pages 8–9)

INVOCATION OF THE SAINTS

O God of our fathers and mothers, who deal with us always in accord with your goodness, do not take your mercy from us, but through their intercession, guide our lives in peace.

Throughout the world your church is dressed in the blood of the martyrs, as if in fine linen and royal purple, and through them cries out to you, O Christ our God:

Send down your compassion upon your people.
Give peace to your commonwealth, and your great mercy to our souls.

+ Glory to the Father, and to the Son, and to the Holy Spirit.
Give rest, O Christ, to the souls of your departed servants, in a place where there is no longer sickness, or sorrow, or sighing; but Life Everlasting.

Now and ever and to the ages of ages. Amen.

Through the intercessions of all the saints, and of the Mother of God, grant us your peace, O Lord, and have mercy upon us. For you alone are merciful.

Lord have mercy   Lord have mercy   *(six times)*

NIGHT PRAYER

Christ our God, who at all times and through every hour, are worshiped and glorified both in heaven and on earth; you who are so patient, full of mercy and compassion; who love the just and show mercy to sinners; who summon all to salvation through the promise of good things to come: Lord, now receive our prayers at this present hour and direct our lives in accordance with your commandments. Sanctify our souls, purify our bodies, correct our minds, clarify our intentions, and deliver us from every calamity, evil, and distress. Stand your holy angels around us that, guided and protected by their ranks, we come into the unity of faith and the knowledge of your unapproachable glory: + For blessed are you to the ages of ages. Amen.

Lord have mercy　　Lord have mercy　　Lord have mercy

DISMISSAL PRAYERS

+ Glory to the Father, and to the Son, and to the Holy Spirit. Now and ever and to the ages of ages. Amen.

More honorable than the Cherubim and incomparably more glorious than the Seraphim, for as a virgin you gave birth to God the Word. Truly the Mother of God, we magnify you.

+ May God have compassion upon us, and bless us; may he let the light of his countenance fall upon us and be merciful to us.

(Or the "Seal")

These final prayers were traditionally said after the night blessing, as a form of final "leave-taking" of the night service, and were recited in a quiet and calm manner by one voice. In the monastic rite, the congregation said all these prayers before leaving church. One might say them all now or select favorites from them.

PRAYER TO THE VIRGIN MOTHER OF GOD

(by Paul, Archimandrite of the Evergetis Monastery in Constantinople)

Immaculate, spotless, incorrupt, undefiled, and radiantly pure Virgin, Lady and Bride of God; by your marvelous conception you united God the Word to humankind and joined our outcast human nature to heavenly things. You are the solitary hope of the hopeless, the support of all who are in trouble, quick to help all who appeal to you, the refuge of all Christians. Do not despise me, a sinner, even though I have wasted my life in shameful imaginings, words, and deeds, and have enslaved myself in the easy addiction of life's pleasures. But since you are the Mother of our Philanthropic God, be philanthropic also and take pity upon me, a transgressor and prodigal. Receive my prayer, even though it is offered to you on unclean lips. Use your boldness as a mother to ask your Son, our Master and Lord, that he would open even to me the loving compassions of his goodness; that he would overlook my countless sins, turn me to repentance, and make of me a God-pleasing fulfiller of his commandments. Be with me always, you who are so compassionate, loving, and merciful, and be throughout this life my powerful protector and helper, defending me against the intrigues of those who hate me. Guide me to salvation, and in the hour of my death look after my poor soul and dispel far from it the gloomy forms of evil demons. In that terrible Day of Judgment, deliver me from eternal punishment, and uphold me as an heir of the ineffable glory of your Son, who is our God. May this be so for me, my Lady, Most Holy Theotokos, because of your advocacy and assistance, and through the grace and love for mankind of your Only Begotten Son, Our Lord and God Jesus Christ, + to whom is due all glory, honor, and worship, with his Father who is without beginning, and his All-Holy, Good, and Life-Creating Spirit, now and ever and to the ages of ages. Amen.

PRAYER TO THE LORD JESUS CHRIST

(by Antiochos, Monk of the Pandektes Monastery)

Master, grant us rest of soul and body as we go now to sleep. Guard us from the gloomy somnolence of sin and from every dark seduction of the night. Calm the turmoil of our obsessions, extinguish the blazing arrows of the evil one so craftily aimed at us. Subdue the rebellions of our flesh, and calm all our earthly and material thoughts. Grant us, O God, a vigilant mind, chaste thought, a sober heart, and sleep that is light and free of all evil dreams. Raise us up again at the hour of prayer, secure in your commandments and holding fast within us the memory of your judgments. Grant that we may sing of your glory all the night long, that we may praise and bless and glorify your all-honorable and majestic name: + of the Father, and of the Son, and of the Holy Spirit, now and ever and to the ages of ages. Amen.

PRAYER TO THE VIRGIN ADVOCATE

Most glorious Ever-Virgin and blessed Mother of God, present our prayer to your Son, who is our God, and pray that, through your advocacy, he will save our souls.

PRAYER OF ST. IOANNIKIOS

+ My hope is the Father.
+ My refuge is the Son.
+ My shelter is the Holy Spirit.
  O Holy Trinity, glory to you.

THEOTOKION: ALL CREATION REJOICES

I commit my every hope to you, O Mother of God. Guard me under your protection.

All creation rejoices in you who are full of grace—both the company of the angels and the human race. Holy Temple and Spiritual Paradise, boast of virgins, from you God was made flesh and became a child, the same who was our God existing before the ages. He made your womb into a throne, making you more spacious than the heavens.

All creation rejoices in you, O Full of Grace. Glory to you.

PRAYER TO THE GUARDIAN ANGEL

Holy angel, watcher over my poor soul and my afflicted life, do not abandon me who am a sinner, and do not leave me because of my fickleness. Leave no room for the spirit of evil to control me by gaining an upper hand over this mortal body, but take me by my poor outstretched hand and lead me into the way of salvation. Holy angel of God, the guardian and protector of my wretched soul and body, forgive me all those things in which I have distressed you over the days of my life and any way I may have sinned this day. Shelter me this coming night and guard me from every abuse of the Adversary, that I may not anger God by any sin. Intercede with the Lord on my behalf to strengthen me in his fear and make me a worthy servant of his goodness. Amen.

LITANY OF INTERCESSION

Lord, we pray for the peace of the world:	Lord have mercy
And for all the church of Christ across the face of the earth	Lord have mercy
For our leaders and mentors, and all who help and encourage us	Lord have mercy
For those who love us, and for those who hate us	Lord have mercy
For those in danger and distress	Lord have mercy
For all those who have asked for our prayers	Lord have mercy
For travelers by land and sea and air	Lord have mercy
For all who lie in sickness	Lord have mercy
For the flourishing of the harvests of the earth	Lord have mercy
For our parents and teachers who have departed this life	Lord have mercy
And for all Christ's faithful who lie asleep in the Lord	Lord have mercy
And for ourselves.	Lord have mercy
	Lord have mercy
	Lord have mercy

SALUTATION OF THE VIRGIN

Theotokos and Virgin, rejoice! Mary, Full of Grace, the Lord is with you. Blessed are you among women and blessed is the fruit of your womb, for you have borne the Savior of our souls.

Awed by the beauty of your virginity and the luminous radiance of your purity, Gabriel called out to you, Theotokos: What fitting hymn of praise can I offer? With what title shall I address you? I am in doubt and stand in awe. Even so, as I was commanded, I cry out to you: Rejoice, O Full of Grace!

THE SEAL

+ Through the prayers of our holy Fathers and Mothers, Lord Jesus Christ our God, have mercy on us and save us. Amen.

A Simplified Office of Morning Prayers

MATINS

(Known in the East as the Rite of Orthros)

The character of Matins is given by the church's desire to proclaim the glorious light of Christ's resurrection, comparing it to the new radiance of the rising of the sun at the beginning of the new day. The exact hour of dawn was the usual time for celebrating this ritual, often after monastics had spent the night in prayer vigil waiting for the sun to rise. Immediately after the Matins, in ancient times, the Eucharist would be celebrated. This pattern is still observed today in many monasteries.

This is quintessentially a "start-of-day" service.

OPENING PRAYER OF BLESSING

+ Blessed is our God. Always now and ever and to the ages of ages. Amen.

(Or the "Seal": Through the prayers of our holy Fathers and Mothers, Lord Jesus Christ our God, have mercy on us and save us.)

TRISAGION PRAYERS

(repeat from pages 8–9)

INVITATORY PRAYER

+ Come let us worship and bow down before God our King.
  (bowing low each time)
+ Come let us worship and bow down before Christ, our King and God.
+ Come let us worship and bow down before Christ himself, our King and our God.

Incense may be offered here before the icons or the cross.

PRAYER OVER THE INCENSE
(said quietly)

+ Incense we offer you, O Christ our God. Accept it at your heavenly throne, and send down upon us, in return, the grace of your Holy Spirit.

THE INITIATORY PSALMS

Psalm 19

May the Lord answer in time of trial;
May the name of Jacob's God protect you.

May he send you help from his shrine
And give you support from Zion.

May he remember all your offerings
And receive your sacrifice with favor.

May he give you your heart's desire
And fulfill every one of your plans.

May we ring out our joy at your victory
And rejoice in the name of our God.

(May the Lord grant all your prayers.)
I am sure now that the Lord will give victory to his anointed,

Will reply from his holy heaven
With the mighty victory of his hand.

Some trust in chariots or horses,
But we in the name of the Lord.

They will collapse and fall,
But we shall hold and stand firm.

Give victory to the king, O Lord,
Give answer on the day we call.

Psalm 20

O Lord, your strength gives joy to the king;
How your saving help makes him glad!

You have granted him his heart's desire;
You have not refused the prayer of his lips.

You came to meet him with the blessings of success,
You set on his head a crown of pure gold.

He asked you for life and this you have given,
Days that will last from age to age.

Your saving help has given him glory.
You have laid upon him majesty and splendor,

You have granted your blessings to him for ever.
You have made him rejoice with the joy of your presence.

The king has put his trust in the Lord:
Through the mercy of the Most High he shall stand firm.

His hand will seek and find all his foes,
His right hand find out those that hate him.

You will burn them like a blazing furnace
On the day when you appear.

And the Lord will destroy them in his anger;
Fire will swallow them up.

You will wipe out their race from the earth
And their children from the sons of men.

Though they plan evil against you,
Though they plot, they shall not prevail.

For you will force them to retreat;
At them you will aim with your bow.

O Lord, arise in your strength;
We shall sing and praise your power.

> + Glory to the Father, and to the Son, and to the Holy Spirit.
> Now and ever and to the ages of ages. Amen.

SONG OF THE CROSS

Lord, save your people and bless your inheritance.
Sustain the people of God against all who hate us.
And by your cross, preserve the commonwealth of Christians.

> + Glory to the Father, and to the Son, and to the Holy Spirit.

RESURRECTION HYMN

O Christ our God, who freely chose to be lifted up on the cross,
Give your mercies to the new race that bears your name.
Gladden with your strength those who govern lawfully,
that by their wisdom we may not fall before those who hate us,

but should always have invincible confidence in your assistance,
our true weapon of peace.

Both now and ever and to the ages of ages. Amen.

HYMN TO THE BLESSED VIRGIN

Look kindly upon our prayers Good and Wondrous Mother of God, for
you are our Mighty Champion who can never be overthrown. Establish
the security of Christian peoples and save those who govern us with your
blessing, granting them success, for you are the Mother of God, and highly
blessed.

THE SIX PSALMS

*In Orthodox practice, the Twelve Prayers of Dawn (below) are said very
quietly by the priest while the choir recites the Six Psalms, or Hexapsalmoi,
aloud. If a small group is praying Matins, one might read the prayers (or
selections from them) while others recite the psalms—or a single person might
care to recite some of the Six Psalms and some of the Twelve Prayers.*

+ Glory to God in the highest, and on earth peace to all of good will.

(three times, bowing low and making the sign of the cross)

Psalm 3

How many are my foes, O Lord!
How many are rising up against me!

How many are saying about me:
"There is no help for him in God."

But you, Lord, are a shield about me,
My glory, who lift up my head.

I cry aloud to the Lord.
He answers from his holy mountain.

I lie down to rest, and I sleep.
I wake, for the Lord upholds me.

I will not fear even thousands of people
Who are ranged on every side against me.

Arise, Lord; save me, my God,
You who strike all my foes on the mouth,

You who break the teeth of the wicked!
O Lord of salvation, bless your people!

Psalm 37

O Lord, do not rebuke me in your anger;
Do not punish me, Lord, in your rage.

Your arrows have sunk deep in me;
Your hand has come down upon me.

Through your anger all my body is sick:
Through my sin, there is no health in my limbs.

My guilt towers higher than my head;
It is a weight too heavy to bear.

My wounds are foul and festering,
The result of my own folly.

I am bowed and brought to my knees.
I go mourning all the day long.

All my frame burns with fever;
All my body is sick.

Spent and utterly crushed,
I cry aloud in anguish of heart.

O Lord, you know all my longing:
My groans are not hidden from you.

My heart throbs, my strength is spent;
The very light has gone from my eyes.

My friends avoid me like a leper;
Those closest to me stand afar off.

Those who plot against my life lay snares;
Those who seek my ruin speak of harm,

Planning treachery all the day long.
But I am like someone deaf who cannot hear,

Like the dumb unable to speak.
I am like someone who hears nothing

In whose mouth is no defense.
I count on you, O Lord:

It is you, Lord God, who will answer.
I pray: "Do not let them mock me,

Those who triumph if my foot should slip."
For I am on the point of falling

And my pain is always before me.
I confess that I am guilty

And my sin fills me with dismay.
My wanton enemies are numberless

And my lying foes are many.
They repay me evil for good

And attack me for seeking what is right.
O Lord, do not forsake me!

My God, do not stay afar off!
Make haste and come to my help,
O Lord, my God, my Savior!

Psalm 62

O God, you are my God, for you I long;
For you my soul is thirsting.

My body pines for you like a dry, weary land without water.
So I gaze on you in the sanctuary

To see your strength and your glory.
For your love is better than life,

My lips will speak your praise.
So I will bless you all my life,

In your name I will lift up my hands.
My soul shall be filled as with a banquet,

My mouth shall praise you with joy.
On my bed I remember you.

On you I muse through the night
For you have been my help;

In the shadow of your wings I rejoice.
My soul clings to you;

Your right hand holds me fast.
Those who seek to destroy my life

Shall go down to the depths of the earth.
They shall be put into the power of the sword

And left as the prey of the jackals.
But the king shall rejoice in God;

(All that swear by him shall be blessed,)
For the mouth of liars shall be silenced.

+ Glory to the Father, and to the Son, and to the Holy Spirit.
   Now and ever and to the ages of ages. Amen.
+ Alleluia, Alleluia, Alleluia, glory to you, O God. *(three times)*

Psalm 87

Lord my God, I call for help by day;
I cry at night before you.

Let my prayer come into your presence.
O turn your ear to my cry.

For my soul is filled with evils;
My life is on the brink of the grave.

I am reckoned as one in the tomb;
I have reached the end of my strength,

Like one alone among the dead;
Like the slain lying in their graves;

Like those you remember no more,
Cut off, as they are, from your hand.

You have laid me in the depths of the tomb,
In places that are dark, in the depths.

Your anger weighs down upon me;
I am drowned beneath your waves.

You have taken away my friends
And made me hateful in their sight.

Imprisoned, I cannot escape;
My eyes are sunken with grief.

I call to you, Lord, all the day long;
To you I stretch out my hands.

Will you work your wonders for the dead?
Will the shades stand and praise you?

Will your love be told in the grave
Or your faithfulness among the dead?

Will your wonders be known in the dark
Or your justice in the land of oblivion?

As for me, Lord, I call to you for help;
In the morning my prayer comes before you.

Lord, why do you reject me?
Why do you hide your face?

Wretched, close to death from my youth,
I have borne your trials; I am numb.

Your fury has swept down upon me;
Your terrors have utterly destroyed me.

They surround me all the day like a flood,
They assail me all together.

Friend and neighbor you have taken away:
My one companion is darkness.

Lord, my God, I call for help by day;
I cry at night before you.

Let my prayer come into your presence.
O turn your ear to my cry.

Psalm 102

My soul, give thanks to the Lord
All my being, bless his holy name.

My soul, give thanks to the Lord
And never forget all his blessings.

It is he who forgives all your guilt,
Who heals every one of your ills,

Who redeems your life from the grave,
Who crowns you with love and compassion,

Who fills your life with good things,
Renewing your youth like an eagle's.

The Lord does deeds of justice,
Gives judgment for all who are oppressed.

He made known his ways to Moses
And his deeds to all Israel.

The Lord is compassion and love,
Slow to anger and rich in mercy.

His wrath will come to an end;
He will not be angry for ever.

He does not treat us according to our sins,
Nor repay us according to our faults.

For as the heavens are high above the earth
So strong is his love for those who fear him.

As far as the east is from the west,
So far does he remove our sins.

As a father has compassion on his child,
The Lord has pity on those who fear him;

For he knows of what we are made,
He remembers that we are dust.

For humans, the days are like grass;
We flower like the flower of the field;

The wind blows and we are gone
And our place never sees us again.

But the love of the Lord is everlasting
Upon those who hold him in fear;

His justice reaches out to children's children
When they keep his covenant in truth,

When they keep his will in their mind.
The Lord has set his sway in heaven

And his kingdom is ruling over all.
Give thanks to the Lord, all his angels,

Mighty in power, fulfilling his word,
Who heed the voice of his word.

Give thanks to the Lord, all his hosts,
His servants who do his will.

Give thanks to the Lord, all his works,
In every place where he rules.
My soul, give thanks to the Lord!

Psalm 142

Lord, listen to my prayer:
Turn your ear to my appeal.

You are faithful, you are just;
Give answer.

Do not call your servant to judgment
For no one is just in your sight.

The enemy pursues my soul;
He has crushed my life to the ground;

He has made me dwell in darkness
Like the dead, long forgotten.

Therefore my spirit fails;
My heart is numb within me.

I remember the days that are past:
I ponder all your works.

I muse on what your hand has wrought
And to you I stretch out my hands.

Like a parched land my soul thirsts for you.
Lord, make haste and answer;
For my spirit fails within me.

Do not hide your face,
Lest I become like those in the grave.

In the morning let me know your love
For I put my trust in you.

Make me know the way I should walk:
To you I lift up my soul.

Rescue me, Lord, from my enemies;
I have fled to you for refuge.

Teach me to do your will
For you, O Lord, are my God.

Let your good spirit guide me
In ways that are level and smooth.

For your name's sake, Lord, save my life;
In your justice save my soul from distress.

In your love make an end of my foes;
Destroy all those who oppress me

For I am your servant, O Lord.

Lord, listen to my prayer;
You are faithful, you are just; give answer
Do not call your servant to judgment.
Let your good spirit guide me
In ways that are level and smooth.

> + Glory to the Father, and to the Son, and to the Holy Spirit.
>   Now and ever and to the ages of ages. Amen.
> + Alleluia, Alleluia, Alleluia, glory to you, O God. *(three times)*

THE TWELVE PRAYERS OF DAWN

If the Morning Office is being celebrated by one or two people at home, a few of these prayers may be chosen from the Twelve and said quietly here, or someone can be designated to offer some or all of the prayers while others recite the Psalm texts.

1. We give you thanks, Lord our God, who have raised us up from our beds and put words of praise into our mouths so that we can worship and call upon your name, and call down your mercies, which we have always experienced throughout our life. Send down your help on those who now stand in the presence of your holy glory, and wait upon your rich mercy, and grant that we may always adore you with reverence and love, with hymns and praise, worshiping your ineffable goodness: + for to you belongs all glory, honor, and worship; to the Father, and to the Son, and to the Holy Spirit, now and ever and to the ages of ages. Amen.

2. Out of the night our spirit rises to you at dawn, our God, for your commandments are a light upon the earth. Teach us to advance in righteousness and holiness and the reverence of God, that we may glorify you, our true God. Stoop down graciously to hear us and be mindful, Lord, of the names of all those who are with us, and pray with us, and save them by your power. Bless your people and sanctify your inheritance. Give peace to the world, to your churches, to your priests, to our rulers, and to all your people: + for blessed and glorified is your all-honorable and majestic name, of the Father, and of the Son, and of the Holy Spirit, now and ever and to the ages of ages. Amen.

3. Out from the night our spirit rises up to you at dawn, our God, for your commandments are a light. Teach us your righteousness, your commandments, and your statutes, O God. Enlighten the eyes of our understanding and prevent us from falling asleep in the death of sin. Dispel all darkness from our hearts. Graciously give to us the Sun of Righteousness, and by your Holy Spirit preserve our life in safety. Guide our steps in the way of peace. Grant that we may look upon the dawn of this new day with joy, that we may gladly raise our morning prayers to you: + for yours is the might, and yours is the kingdom, and the power, and the glory, of the Father, and of the Son, and of the Holy Spirit, now and ever and to the ages of ages. Amen.

4. Master, Holy and Incomprehensible God, who commanded the light to shine out of darkness, who have refreshed us by the slumber of the night and now have raised us up to glorify your goodness through our prayers: as we call upon your tenderness of heart, accept us who worship you and give you thanks to the best of our ability, and grant us all our petitions which are useful to salvation. Make us children of the light and children of the day, heirs of your everlasting blessings. Be mindful, Lord, in the multitude of your mercies, of all the people of God joined with us in prayer and all our innumerable brothers and sisters on land, or sea, and in every place of your dominion, for all are in need of your philanthropy and your help; and grant to all of them your great mercy, that being preserved in safety of soul and body, we may always and confidently glorify your wondrous and blessed name, + of the Father, and of the Son, and of the Holy Spirit, now and ever and to the ages of ages. Amen.

5. Treasury of the Good, Everlasting Spring, Holy Father who work wonders, All-Powerful and Almighty One, we worship you and pray to you, calling on your mercies and your compassions to help and defend us who are so poor. Remember us, your servants, Lord; receive our morning prayers as incense before you and let none of us be found deficient, but clothe us round with your mercies. Be mindful, Lord, of those who watch and sing to the glory of your Only Begotten Son and your Holy Spirit. Be their helper and their support. Receive their prayers on your heavenly and spiritual altar: for you are our God, and to you we ascribe glory, + to the Father, and to the Son, and to the Holy Spirit, now and ever and to the ages of ages. Amen.

6. We give you thanks, Lord God of our salvation, for all that you have done to save us. Let us always look up to you as the Savior and Benefactor of our souls, for you have refreshed us with rest in the night and raised us up from our beds to stand and worship your honorable name. And so, Lord, we pray you to give us grace and power that we may be worthy to sing to you with understanding, and pray unceasingly in fear and trembling, and to work out our salvation through the assistance of your Christ. Be mindful, Lord, of those of those who cry out to you in the darkness. Hear them and have mercy, and beat down under their feet their invisible and hostile foes: for you are the King of Peace, and the Savior of our souls, and to you we ascribe glory, + to the Father, and to the Son, and to the Holy Spirit, now and ever and to the ages of ages. Amen.

7. God and Father of our Lord Jesus Christ, you have raised us up from our beds and gathered us together at this hour of prayer: grant us grace in opening our mouths, and accept our offerings of thanks, according to our ability to make them, and instruct us in your statutes, for we do not know how we ought to pray, unless you guide us, Lord, by your Holy Spirit. And so, we ask you: forgive, remit, and pardon any sins we may have committed to this present hour, whether by word or deed or thought, whether voluntary or involuntary; for if you should mark our transgressions, Lord, who could ever stand? But with you is redemption; for you are holy, a mighty helper, and the defender of our life, and our song shall ever be to you, + for blessed and glorified is the power of your kingdom, of the Father, and of the Son, and of the Holy Spirit, now and ever and to the ages of ages. Amen.

8. Lord God, you have driven away the sluggishness of our sleep and given us the call to gather in the lifting up of our hands, even in the nighttime, so as to confess your holy judgments. Receive our prayers, petitions, confessions, and adorations before the dawn, and grant to us, our God, a faith unashamed, a hope that is unwavering, a love that is true. Bless all our going out and our coming in, all our deeds and works, our words and thoughts. And grant that we may come to the beginning of this day praising and singing and blessing the goodness of your ineffable kindness; + for blessed is your all-holy name, and glorified is the kingdom of the Father, and of the Son, and of the Holy Spirit, now and ever and to the ages of ages. Amen.

9. Philanthropic Lord, illumine our hearts with the pure light of your divine knowledge and open the eyes of our mind to understand your gospel teachings. Plant within us reverence for your blessed commandments so that we may be able to cast aside our hedonism and enter upon a spiritual manner of living, thinking and doing those things that are pleasing in your sight; for you are our sanctification and illumination, and to you we ascribe glory, + to the Father, and to the Son, and to the Holy Spirit, now and ever and to the ages of ages. Amen.

10. Lord our God, you have granted to mortals pardon through repentance and have set the repentance of the prophet David before us as an example of how to acknowledge our sin and how to make that confession which leads to forgiveness. Master, have mercy on us, yourself, according to your abundant mercy, and do not remember the many great iniquities into which we have fallen. Blot out our transgressions according to the multitude of your mercies. Against you, we have sinned, Lord, and you alone know the hidden and secret things of our hearts, and you alone have the power to forgive sins. But since it was you who created a clean heart within us, and established us with your guiding Spirit, and revealed to us the joy of your salvation, then do not cast us away from your presence. Since you are a philanthropic God of great goodness, graciously allow us, even to our last breath, to offer you the sacrifice of righteousness and the oblation upon your holy altars: through the mercies and compassion and philanthropic love of your Only Begotten Son, + with whom you are blessed, together with your All-Holy, Good, and Life-Giving Spirit, now and ever and to the ages of ages. Amen.

11. O God, our God, who have willed into being all rational beings endowed with speech, we pray and beseech you to receive our praises, which we offer you according to our ability, along with those of all your creatures, and to grant us in return the rich gifts of your goodness; for to you every knee shall bow, whether in the heavens, or on the earth, or under the earth; and every creature that has breath sings to your ineffable glory; for you alone are the true and most merciful God, and all the powers of heaven praise you, + and we too ascribe glory, to the Father, and to the Son, and to the Holy Spirit, now and ever and to the ages of ages. Amen.

12. We praise you, we hymn you, we bless you, we give thanks to you, God of our Fathers and Mothers, for you have brought us safely through the shadows of night and once again have shown to us the light of day. We ask of your goodness that you would be gracious to our sins and receive our prayer because of your great tenderness of heart, for we take refuge with you, the Merciful and All-Powerful God. Illumine our hearts with your true Sun of Righteousness; enlighten our mind and guard all our senses, that walking honestly, as in the day and in the path of your commandments, we may attain to everlasting life (for with you is the fountain of life), and might be made worthy of enjoying the unapproachable light; for you are our God, + and to you we ascribe glory, to the Father, and to the Son, and to the Holy Spirit, now and ever and to the ages of ages. Amen.

Matins resumes with the "Great Litany of Intercession."

THE GREAT LITANY OF INTERCESSION

+ In peace let us pray to the Lord.   Lord have mercy

+ For the peace from above and the salvation of
our souls, let us pray to the Lord.   Lord have mercy

+ For the peace of the whole world, the welfare of
the holy churches of God, and the unity of all,
let us pray to the Lord.   Lord have mercy

+ For those who pray with us, for those who serve in
government in church or state, and for all who
reverence God, let us pray to the Lord.   Lord have mercy

+ For healthful weather, for abundance of the fruits
of the earth, and for peaceful times, let us pray
to the Lord.   Lord have mercy

+ For all who travel, for all who suffer or are in
distress of any kind, let us pray to the Lord.   Lord have mercy

+ That we and all those we love may be saved
from all trouble and dangers, let us pray
to the Lord.   Lord have mercy

+ O God, help us, save us, have mercy on us, and
always keep us.   Lord have mercy

+ Calling to mind our most holy, blessed, and glorious
Lady, the Mother of God and Ever-Virgin Mary, with
all the saints, we commend ourselves, and each
another, and all our lives, to Christ our God.   To you, O Lord.

+ For to you are due all glory, honor, and worship:
  To the Father, the Son, and the Holy Spirit,
  Now and ever and to the ages of ages.   Amen.

THE MORNING HYMNS

(A) *STICHERA*, OR HYMN VERSES, ON "GOD IS THE LORD"

God is the Lord and has revealed himself to us.

Blessed is he who comes in the name of the Lord.
Confess to the Lord and call upon his holy name.

God is the Lord and has revealed himself to us.
All the nations encircled me, but in the Lord's name I drove them back.
This is the work of the Lord, and it is wonderful in our sight.

God is the Lord and has revealed himself to us.
Blessed is he who comes in the name of the Lord.

(B) HYMN OF THE RESURRECTION

The stone was sealed by the rulers in Jerusalem,
And the soldiers guarded your immaculate body.
But on the third day, our Savior,
You rose to give life to the world.

And so the Heavenly Powers cry out to you, O Giver of Life:
Glory to your resurrection, O Christ, glory to your kingdom.
Glory to your economy of salvation, Only Lover of Mankind.

+ Glory to the Father, and to the Son, and to the Holy Spirit.

(C) PRAYER TO THE SAINT OF THE DAY

Holy Father *(Mother)*, Saint –X–
You were a fragrant sign of Christ's graciousness
In all that you said and did.
Now sharing in his glory, intercede with the Lord
For us who call upon you in prayer.

Now and ever and to the ages of ages. Amen.

THEOTOKION—HYMN TO THE MOTHER OF GOD

When Gabriel's greeting flashed upon you, O Virgin,
At the very sound the Lord of All took flesh, in you,
The Holy Ark, as righteous David called you.
And then you were revealed as "Wider-than-the Heavens"
For you enfolded your Creator. Glory to him who dwelt
   in you.
Glory to him who came forth from you.
Glory to him who by your giving-birth has given
us our freedom.

THE PSALM VERSES

Here the monastics recite further psalms in the formal Church Offices (usually Pss. 9–16 LXX). If, on occasion, it is desired to extend this morning prayer, one can add in extra psalms here from the Psalter. Psalms 5, 91, 92, 94, and 102 (LXX) are especially suitable for Morning Prayers.

Psalm 10

In the Lord I have taken my refuge.
How can you say to my soul:
"Fly like a bird to its mountain.

See the wicked bracing their bow;
They are fixing their arrows on the string

To shoot upright men in the dark.
Foundations once destroyed, what can the just do?"

The Lord is in his holy temple,
The Lord, whose throne is in heaven.

His eyes look down on the world;
His gaze tests mortal men.

The Lord tests the just and the wicked;
The lover of violence he hates.

He sends fire and brimstone on the wicked;
He sends a scorching wind as their lot.

The Lord is just and loves justice;
The upright shall see his face.

HYMN OF MERCY

Praise the name of the Lord, you servants of the Lord.
Alleluia. Alleluia. Alleluia.
Praised be the Lord from Zion, he who dwells in Jerusalem.
Alleluia. Alleluia. Alleluia.
Give thanks to the Lord for he is good. His mercy endures forever.
Alleluia. Alleluia. Alleluia.

BEATITUDES OF THE RESURRECTION

Blessed are you, O Lord; teach me your statutes.
The ranks of angels were amazed to see you down among the dead,
You who had broken death's power,
Raising Adam up once more,
And freeing us all along with him.
Blessed are you, O Lord; teach me your statutes.
The radiant angel spoke to the women in the tomb:
Do not drop your tears in these ointments.
Look at his tomb and be glad of heart.
For the Lord has risen from the dead.
Blessed are you, O Lord; teach me your statutes.

A READING FROM THE HOLY GOSPEL[4]

Then the eleven disciples went to Galilee, to the mountain to which Jesus
had directed them. When they saw him they worshiped him; but some of
them had doubts. And Jesus coming up to them said this: "All authority
in heaven and on earth has been given to me. And so, go out and make
disciples of all nations, baptizing them in the name of the Father and of

the Son and of the Holy Spirit, teaching them to observe all the things I have commanded you. And know this: I am with you always, even to the end of the age." (Matt. 28:16–20)

HYMN OF THE RESURRECTION

In that we have seen the resurrection of Christ, let us bow down before the Holy Lord Jesus, Only Sinless One. We worship your cross, O Christ, and we praise and glorify your holy resurrection. For you are our God, and we confess none other. Come, you faithful, and let us adore Christ's holy resurrection. For by the cross joy has come into the world. Ever blessing the Lord, let us sing of his resurrection, for by enduring the cross he put death itself to death.

THE CANON OF MATINS *(abbreviated)*

ODE 1

Irmos	Your right hand has triumphed, as befits our God,
	Your might has been glorified, Immortal One,
	Glory to your holy resurrection, Lord.

Troparion	You, whose spotless hands made me,
	And formed me in the beginning;
	Hands that were stretched out upon the cross,
	Call me up from the corruption of clay.
	Glory to your holy resurrection, Lord.

+ Glory to the Father, and to the Son, and to the Holy Spirit.
Now and ever and to the ages of ages. Amen.

Theotokion   Hail, Fountain of Grace!
Hail, Ladder and Gate of Heaven!
Hail, the Lamp, the Vase of Gold, the Unquarried
Mountain,
Who bore in your womb Christ, who gives life
to the world.

Katavasia   I will open my mouth, and the Spirit shall inspire it,
And I shall sing my canticle to the Queen and Mother
Radiantly will I keep her feast;
Joyfully will I praise her wonders.

(Ode 2 is always omitted in church practice.)

ODE 3

Irmos   Lord, you know indeed the weakness of our mortal state,
For in compassion you received its form.
Clothe me in power from above that I may cry to you:
Glory to your holy resurrection, Lord.

ODE 4

Irmos　　Abbakum saw you in prophetic vision, O Mother of God,
As a Mountain overshadowed with divine grace;
And he cried out: From you shall come the Holy One
　of Israel,
Glory to your holy resurrection, Lord.

ODE 5

Irmos　　You have illumined the ends of the earth, O Christ,
With the brightness of your presence;
Giving joy to the world through your cross;
So now, enlighten the hearts of your faithful
With the light of the knowledge of God.
Glory to your holy resurrection, Lord.

ODE 6

Irmos　　A bottomless pit yawns before us,
And there is no one else who can save us.
Save your people, O God, our strength and salvation.
Glory to your holy resurrection, Lord.

ODE 7

Irmos　　Mother of God, the faithful see you as the holy fire.
For as the Most High saved the children in the furnace,
So he made man afresh within your womb,
The God of our Fathers, praised and most glorious.
Glory to your holy resurrection, Lord.

ODE 8

Irmos   In the furnace, as if in a crucible,
The three children shone brighter than gold
In the beauty of their holiness,
And cried out: Bless the Lord, all his works!
Praise and exalt him to the ages!
Glory to your holy resurrection, Lord.

THE MAGNIFICATIONS

The Theotokos and Mother of the Light, Let us honor with song!

God is the Lord and has revealed himself to us.
Blessed is he who comes in the name of the Lord.
+ Glory to the Father, and to the Son, and to the Holy Spirit.
Now and ever and to the ages of ages. Amen.
Alleluia, Alleluia, Alleluia, glory to you, O Lord. *(three times)*

My soul magnifies the Lord, and my spirit rejoices in God my savior.
For he has looked on the lowliness of his handmaiden.
Behold, from henceforth all generations shall call me blessed.

More honorable than the Cherubim and incomparably more glorious than the Seraphim, for as a virgin you gave birth to God the Word himself.

For he that is mighty has done great things for me, and holy is his name.
His mercy is on those who fear him, from generation to generation.

More honorable than the Cherubim and incomparably more glorious than the Seraphim, for as a virgin you gave birth to God the Word himself.

He has shown the strength of his arm;

He has scattered the proud in the conceit of their hearts.

He has cast down the mighty from their thrones and has exalted
the lowly.

He has filled the hungry with good things, sent the rich away empty.

More honorable than the Cherubim and incomparably more glorious
than the Seraphim, for as a virgin you gave birth to God the
Word himself.

Mindful of his mercy, he has come to the help of Israel his servant,

As he promised to our fathers, to Abraham and his sons forever.

Most Blessed are you, Virgin Mother of God, for the one who was born of
you has taken hell as captive. Adam has been restored; the curse has been
annulled. Eve has been set free; death has died; and we have been made
alive once more. And so, in our hymn to you, we cry aloud: Blessed is
Christ our God, who was pleased to do all this. Glory to you.

CANON OF RESURRECTION *(conclusion)*

Incense is often offered here to the icon of the Mother of God.

ODE 9

Irmos   The burning bush, which was never consumed,
             Was a mystic symbol of your pure conception;
             And so, Mother of God, we entreat you:
             Extinguish within us the blazing fire of our obsessions
             That we may unceasingly magnify you.
             Glory to your holy resurrection, Lord.

+ Glory to the Father, and to the Son, and to the Holy Spirit.
Now and ever and to the ages of ages. Amen.

Theotokion   Hail, Spring of Ever-Living Water!
             Hail, Paradise of Delights!
             Hail, Strong Bulwark of the faithful!
             Hail, Maiden, joy of all the world!
             Through whom arose for us,
             The God of our Fathers, praised and most glorious.

THE GREAT DOXOLOGY

Glory to you who have shown us the Light.

Glory to God in the highest, and on earth peace and goodwill
    among men.
We praise you, we bless you, we worship you, we glorify you,
We give you thanks for your great glory.
O Lord our King, Heavenly God, Almighty Father:
O Lord, Only Begotten Son, Jesus Christ, and Holy Spirit;
O Lord God, Lamb of God, Son of the Father,
Who takes away the sin of the world,
Have mercy on us, you who take away the sin of the world.
You who sit at the right hand of the Father,
Receive our prayer, and have mercy on us.
For you alone are holy, you alone are the Lord, Jesus Christ,
To the glory of God the Father. Amen.

Every day I will bless you, and will praise your name forever;
Yes, forever and ever.
Grant, Lord, to keep us this day without sin.

Blessed are you, Lord; teach me your statutes.
Blessed are you, Master; make me understand your statutes.
Blessed are you, Holy One; illuminate me with your statutes.

Lord, you have been our refuge from one generation to the next.
I said, Lord have mercy on me; heal my soul for I have sinned
    against you.
Lord, I have fled to you, teach me to do your will, for you are my God.
For with you is the source of life, and in your light we shall see light.
Continue your mercy to those who know you.

FINAL MORNING PRAYER

Holy Lord, who dwell on high and with an all-seeing eye look on the whole of creation, having regard for the humble of heart, we have bowed down body and soul before you. We beseech you, Holy of Holies, to stretch out your unseen hand from your holy dwelling place and bless us all. And if we have sinned in any way, whether voluntarily or involuntarily, forgive us; for you are a good God who loves mankind, who unfailingly grants to us your earthly and heavenly benefits and ceaselessly shows us your mercy and saves us; + and to you we ascribe glory, to the Father, and to the Son, and to the Holy Spirit, now and ever and to the ages of ages. Amen.

THE SEAL

+ Through the prayers of our holy Fathers and Mothers, Lord Jesus Christ our God, have mercy on us and save us. Amen.

Prayers for Late Morning
THE OFFICE OF THE FIRST HOUR

Traditionally said at 6:00 AM in the monasteries (the "first hour" of daylight), this Office is suitable for marking out a time of prayer in the late morning, and its companion piece (the Third Hour), for a brief service of prayers in the middle of the day.

OPENING PRAYER OF BLESSING

+ Blessed is our God. Always now and ever and to the ages of ages. Amen.

(Or the "Seal")

Glory to you, our God, glory to you.

TRISAGION PRAYERS
(repeat from pages 8–9)

INVITATORY PRAYER

+ Come let us worship and bow down before God our King.
(bowing low each time)
+ Come let us worship and bow down before Christ, our King and God.
+ Come let us worship and bow down before Christ himself, our King and our God.

THE THREE PSALMS[5]

Psalm 5

To my words give ear, O Lord, give heed to my groaning.
Attend to the sound of my cries, my King and my God.

It is you whom I invoke, O Lord. In the morning you hear me;
In the morning I offer you my prayer, watching and waiting.

You are no God who loves evil; no sinner is your guest.
The boastful shall not stand their ground before your face.

You hate all who do evil; you destroy all who lie.
The deceitful and the bloodthirsty the Lord detests.

But I through the greatness of your love have access to your house.
I bow down before your holy temple, filled with awe.

Lead me, Lord, in your justice, because of those who lie in wait;
Make clear your way before me.

No truth can be found in their mouths, their heart is all mischief,
Their throat a wide-open grave, all honey their speech.

Declare them guilty, O God. Let them fail in their designs.
Drive them out for their many offenses, for they have defied you.

All those you protect shall be glad and ring out their joy.
You shelter them; in you they rejoice, those who love your name.

It is you who bless the just.
You surround them with favor as with a shield.

Psalm 89

O Lord, you have been our refuge from one generation to the next.
Before the mountains were born or the earth or the world brought forth,

You are God, without beginning or end.
You turn mortals back to dust and say: "Go back, Adam's child."

To your eyes a thousand years are like yesterday, come and gone,
No more than a watch in the night.

You sweep us away like a dream, like grass which springs up
    in the morning.
In the morning it springs up and flowers: by evening it withers and fades.

So we are destroyed in your anger, struck with terror in your fury.
Our guilt lies open before you; our secrets in the light of your face.

All our days pass away in your anger. Our life is over like a sigh.
Our span is seventy years, or eighty for those who are strong.

And most of these are emptiness and pain. They pass swiftly and
    we are gone.
Who understands the power of your anger and fears the strength of
    your fury?

Make us know the shortness of our life that we may gain wisdom
    of heart.
Lord, relent! Is your anger for ever? Show pity to your servants.

In the morning, fill us with your love; we shall exult and rejoice
    all our days.
Give us joy to balance our affliction for the years when we
    knew misfortune.

Show forth your work to your servants; let your glory shine
   on their children.
Let the favor of the Lord be upon us: Give success to the work
   of our hands.
(Give success to the work of our hands.)

Psalm 100

My song is of mercy and justice; I sing to you, O Lord.
I will walk in the way of perfection. O when, Lord, will you come?

I will walk with blameless heart within my house;
I will not set before my eyes whatever is base.

I will hate the ways of the crooked; they shall not be my friends.
The false-hearted must keep far away; the wicked I disown.

Whoever slanders their neighbor in secret I will bring to silence.
People of proud looks and haughty heart I will never endure.

I look to the faithful in the land that they may dwell with me.
All who walk in the way of perfection, shall be my friends.

No one who practices deceit shall live within my house.
No one who utters lies shall stand before my eyes.

Morning by morning I will silence all the wicked in the land,
Uprooting from the Lord's city all who do evil.

   + Glory to the Father, and to the Son, and to the Holy Spirit.
     Now and ever and to the ages of ages. Amen.
   + Alleluia, Alleluia, Alleluia, glory to you, O God. *(three times)*

HYMN VERSES

+ Attend to the sound of my cries, my King and my God.
   In the morning hear me. *(bowing low at each verse and making the sign of the cross)*

   To my words give ear, O Lord. Give heed to my groaning.

+ Attend to the sound of my cries, my King and my God.
   In the morning hear me.
   It is you whom I invoke, O Lord.
   In the morning you hear me.

+ Attend to the sound of my cries, my King and my God.
   In the morning hear me.

+ Glory to the Father, and to the Son, and to the Holy Spirit.
   Now and ever and to the ages of ages. Amen.

SONG TO THE VIRGIN

What shall we call you who are full of grace?
A Heaven: for from you shone out the Sun of Righteousness;
A Paradise: for from your bud came the Flower of Immortality;
A Virgin: for you have remained immaculate;
A Pure Mother: for you have held a son in your embrace, who is the
   God of all.
Intercede with him to save our souls.

VERSES ON THE PSALMS[6]

Direct my steps in accordance with your word,
And let no evil rule over me.

Deliver me from slandering tongues,
And I will keep your commandments.

Let your face shine on your servant,
And teach me your statutes.

Fill my mouth with your praise, O Lord,
And I will sing of your glory and majesty all the day long.

Then on a weekday, say a prayer to the saint of the day or a patron saint.
The saint of the day can be referenced from a liturgical calendar.

PRAYER TO THE SAINT OF THE DAY

Holy Father *(Mother)*, Saint –X–
You were a fragrant sign of Christ's graciousness
In all that you said and did.
Now sharing in his glory, intercede with the Lord
For us who call upon you in prayer.

But on a Sunday say the following "Hymn of the Resurrection" as well:

HYMN OF THE RESURRECTION

Christ our God, and Great Lover of our race,
You took our human form upon yourself,
To suffer for our sake upon the cross.
Save us, Lord, by your holy resurrection.

Lord have mercy   Lord have mercy   Lord have mercy

THEOTOKION—PRAYER TO THE BLESSED VIRGIN MARY

More Honorable than the Cherubim,
And incomparably more glorious than the Seraphim,
For as a virgin you gave birth to God the Word.
Truly the Mother of God, we magnify you.

CONCLUDING PRAYER

Christ our God, who at all times and through every hour, are worshiped and glorified both in heaven and on earth; you who are so patient, full of mercy and compassion; who love the just and show mercy to sinners; who summon all to salvation through the promise of good things to come: Lord, now receive our prayers at this present hour, and direct our lives in accordance with your commandments. Sanctify our souls, purify our bodies, correct our minds, clarify our intentions, and deliver us from every calamity, evil, and distress. Stand your holy angels around us that, guided and protected by their ranks, we come into the unity of faith and the knowledge of your unapproachable glory, + for blessed are you to the ages of ages. Amen.

+ Glory to the Father, and to the Son, and to the Holy Spirit.
Now and ever and to the ages of ages. Amen.

FINAL BLESSING

+ May God have compassion on us and bless us;
May he show the light of his countenance to us, and be merciful to us. Amen.

(or the "Seal")

Prayers for Midday
THE OFFICE OF THE THIRD HOUR

OPENING PRAYER OF BLESSING

+ Blessed is our God. Always now and ever and to the ages of ages. Amen.

(or the "Seal")

Glory to you, our God, glory to you.

TRISAGION PRAYERS
(repeat from pages 8–9)

INVITATORY PRAYER

+ Come let us worship and bow down before God our King.
(bowing low each time)
+ Come let us worship and bow down before Christ, our King and God.
+ Come let us worship and bow down before Christ himself, our King and our God.

Psalm 16

Lord, hear a cause that is just;
pay heed to my cry.

Turn your ear to my prayer:
no deceit is on my lips.

From you, may my judgment come forth.
Your eyes discern the truth.

You search my heart, you visit me by night.
You test me and you find in me no wrong.

My words are not sinful as others' words.
I kept from violence because of your word,

I kept my feet firmly in your paths;
There was no faltering in my steps.

I am here and I call, you will hear me, O God.
Turn your ear to me; hear my words.

Display your great love, you whose right hand saves
Your friends from those who rebel against them.

Guard me as the apple of your eye.
Hide me in the shadow of your wings,
From the violent attack of the wicked.

My foes encircle me with deadly intent.
Their hearts tight shut, their mouths speak proudly.

They advance against me, and now they surround me.
Their eyes are watching to strike me to the ground,

As though they were lions ready to claw
Or like some young lion crouched in hiding.

Lord, arise, confront them, strike them down!
Let your sword rescue my soul from the wicked;

Let your hand, O Lord, rescue me from those
Whose reward is in this present life.

You give them their fill of your treasures;
they rejoice in abundance of offspring
and leave their wealth to their children.

As for me, in my justice I shall see your face
and be filled, when I awake, with the sight of your glory.

Psalm 24

To you, O Lord, I lift up my soul.
I trust you, let me not be disappointed;

Do not let my enemies triumph.
Those who hope in you shall not be disappointed,
But only those who wantonly break faith.

Lord, make me know your ways.
Lord, teach me your paths.

Make me walk in your truth, and teach me:
For you are God my savior.

In you I hope all the day long
Because of your goodness, O Lord.

Remember your mercy, Lord,
And the love you have shown from of old.

Do not remember the sins of my youth.
In your love remember me.

The Lord is good and upright.
He shows the path to those who stray.

He guides the humble in the right path.
He teaches his way to the poor.

His ways are faithfulness and love
for those who keep his covenant and law.

Lord, for the sake of your name
Forgive my guilt, for it is great.

If anyone fears the Lord,
He will reveal the right path to choose.

Your soul shall live in happiness
And your children shall possess the land.

The Lord's friendship is for those who revere him;
To them he reveals his covenant.

My eyes are always on the Lord;
For he rescues my feet from the snare.

Turn to me and have mercy
For I am lonely and poor.

Relieve the anguish of my heart
And set me free from my distress.

See my affliction and my toil
And take all my sins away.

See how many are my foes;
How violent their hatred for me.

Preserve my life and rescue me.
Do not disappoint me, you are my refuge.

May innocence and uprightness protect me:
For my hope is in you, O Lord.

Redeem Israel, O God,
From all its distress.

Psalm 50

Have mercy on me, God, in your kindness.
In your compassion blot out my offense.

O wash me more and more from my guilt
And cleanse me from my sin.

My offenses truly I know them;
My sin is always before me.

Against you, you alone, have I sinned;
What is evil in your sight I have done.

That you may be justified when you give sentence
And be without reproach when you judge,

O see, in guilt I was born,
A sinner was I conceived.

Indeed you love truth in the heart;
Then in the secret of my heart teach me wisdom.

O purify me, then I shall be clean;
O wash me, I shall be whiter than snow.

Make me hear rejoicing and gladness,
That the bones you have crushed may thrill.

From my sins turn away your face
And blot out all my guilt.

A pure heart create for me, O God,
Put a steadfast spirit within me.

Do not cast me away from your presence,
Nor deprive me of your holy spirit.

Give me again the joy of your help;
With a spirit of fervor sustain me,

That I may teach transgressors your ways
And sinners may return to you.

O rescue me, God, my helper,
And my tongue shall ring out your goodness.

O Lord, open my lips
And my mouth shall declare your praise.

For in sacrifice you take no delight,
Burnt offering from me you would refuse,

My sacrifice, a contrite spirit.
A humbled, contrite heart you will not spurn.

In your goodness, show favor to Zion:
Rebuild the walls of Jerusalem.

Then you will be pleased with lawful sacrifice,
(Burnt offerings wholly consumed),
Then you will be offered young bulls on your altar.

> + Glory to the Father, and to the Son, and to the Holy Spirit.
>   Now and ever and to the ages of ages. Amen.
> + Alleluia, Alleluia, Alleluia, glory to you, O God. *(three times)*

HYMN OF THE THIRD HOUR

O Lord, who at the Third Hour,
Sent down your Holy Spirit upon the apostles:
Do not take the same from us, O Good One,
But renew him within us who pray to you. *(bowing low)*

+ A clean heart create for me, O God.
Put a steadfast spirit within me.

O Lord, who at the Third Hour
Sent down your Holy Spirit upon the apostles:
Do not take the same from us, O Good One,
But renew him within us who pray to you. *(bowing low)*
+ Do not cast me away from your presence,
Nor deprive me of your Holy Spirit.

O Lord, who at the Third Hour
Sent down your Holy Spirit upon the apostles:
Do not take the same from us, O Good One,
But renew him within us who pray to you. *(bowing low)*

+ Glory to the Father, and to the Son, and to the Holy Spirit.
Now and ever and to the ages of ages. Amen.

THEOTOKION—HYMN TO THE VIRGIN

Mother of God, you are the true vine
Whose bud produced the Fruit of Life.
Intercede with him, we pray,
With all the apostles and the saints,
That he will have mercy upon our souls.

Blessed is the Lord our God;
Blessed is the Lord day by day.

The God of our salvation shall prosper us along the way.
Our God is the God of salvation.

RESURRECTION HYMN

O Christ, you rose as God, in glory, from the tomb;
Raising up the entire world at your side.

Mortal nature hymns you as its God,
For death has been destroyed.

Adam rejoices, O Master,
And Eve, now ransomed from her bonds, cries out to you:

O Christ you have brought resurrection to all mankind.

Lord have mercy   Lord have mercy   Lord have mercy *(four times)*

PRAYER FOR MERCY

Christ our God, who at all times and through every hour are worshiped
and glorified both in heaven and on earth; you who are so patient, full of
mercy and compassion; who love the just and show mercy to sinners; who
summon all to salvation through the promise of good things to come:
Lord, now receive our prayers at this present hour and direct our lives in
accordance with your commandments. Sanctify our souls, purify our bodies, correct our minds, clarify our intentions, and deliver us from every
calamity, evil, and distress. Stand your holy angels around us that, guided
and protected by their ranks, we may come into the unity of faith and the
knowledge of your unapproachable glory: + for blessed are you to the ages
of ages. Amen.

Lord have mercy   Lord have mercy   Lord have mercy

+ Glory to the Father, and to the Son, and to the Holy Spirit.
  Now and ever and to the ages of ages. Amen.

More honorable than the Cherubim and incomparably more glorious than the Seraphim, for as a virgin you gave birth to God the Word; truly the Mother of God, we magnify you.

O Christ, the True Light, which illumines and sanctifies everyone, coming into the world: Let the light of your countenance be signed upon us, that in it we may behold the light ineffable. Guide our footsteps securely in the keeping of your commandments; + through the intercessions of your All-Immaculate Mother, and of all your saints. Amen.

FINAL BLESSING

+ May God have compassion on us and bless us;
  May he let the light of his countenance fall upon us and be merciful to us. Amen.

(or the "Seal")

PART 2

Rituals and Services of Prayer for Different Occasions

This book has been intended to help prayer in the domestic situation. At times occasions can arise where the distinction between private/domestic and formal/public prayer becomes blurred. There may be an illness or a trouble in the home which calls out to several family members at once, or the presence of a sick or dying person at home can often bring up a need for a ritual of prayer more suitable for the family gathered together, or with friends present also. And so the following short rituals have been set out as a suggested guide for times when a family might need a service of prayer to bring them together. They are based upon the ancient church rituals, but do not presume the presence of a priest or minister which is not always so easily arranged in this day and age. One person can lead the whole service; and just as easily, many different parts of the service can be assigned to different friends or family members. Talking over the service together before doing it as a common act of prayer is always a good idea: and those taking part in it can mentally mark their respective parts.

Ritual for the Blessing of a Home

Local ordained clergy will usually be more than glad to lead a service of house blessing for a family that asks. If you wish to call God's blessing on your home yourself, or with friends: prepare a small table in the main room of the house, if possible facing eastward, and lay on it a copy of the Gospels, a cross or icon, and a lighted candle. If you have some holy water (bring it home from church or ask a priest for some), use this for blessing all the various rooms, but if you cannot find blessed water, use incense that you have blessed with the prayer for blessing (see below). Beforehand, with the water (or with a little olive oil) mark a small sign of the cross inside the four external walls of the house or apartment in the four geographical faces (north, south, east, and west) at door height, saying each time: "Lord, bless and protect this house always by the sign of the holy cross." Gather some close friends together to celebrate your house blessing, and after the initial prayers and Scripture readings, all make a procession around the house, if there is room, following the leader of the service, as each room is blessed by sprinkling holy water or by lifting up the incense in the form of a cross in each room.

THE OPENING BLESSING

+ In the name of the Father, and of the Son, and of the Holy Spirit. Amen.

Glory to you, our God, glory to you.

(or the "Seal")

THE TRISAGION PRAYERS
(repeat from pages 8–9)

INVITATORY PRAYER

+ Come let us worship and bow down before God our King.
(bowing low each time)

+ Come let us worship and bow down before Christ, our King and God.

+ Come let us worship and bow down before Christ himself, our King and our God.

Psalm 90
(Alternate the Psalm verses in two groups.)

One who dwells in the shelter of the Most High
And abides in the shade of the Almighty

Says to the Lord: "My refuge,
My stronghold, my God in whom I trust!"

It is he who will free you from the snare of the fowler
Who seeks to destroy you;

He will conceal you with his pinions
And under his wings you will find refuge.

You will not fear the terror of the night
Nor the arrow that flies by day,

Nor the plague that prowls in the darkness
Nor the scourge that lays waste at noon.

A thousand may fall at your side,
Ten thousand fall at your right,

You, it will never approach;
His faithfulness is buckler and shield.

Your eyes have only to look
To see how the wicked are repaid,

You who have said: "Lord, my refuge!"
And have made the Most High your dwelling.

Upon you no evil shall fall,
No plague approach where you dwell.

For you has he commanded his angels,
To keep you in all your ways.

They shall bear you upon their hands
Lest you strike your foot against a stone.

On the lion and the viper you will tread
And trample the young lion and the dragon.

One who clings to me in love, I will set free;
Protect the one who knows my name.

Call out and I shall answer: "I am with you."
I will save you in distress and give you glory.

With length of days I will content you.
I shall let you see my saving power.

+ Glory to the Father, and to the Son, and to the Holy Spirit.
  Now and ever and to the ages of ages. Amen.

+ Alleluia, Alleluia, Alleluia, glory to you, O God. *(three times)*

VERSES OF BENEDICTION

If there is incense:

+ Incense we offer you, O Christ our God. Accept it at your heavenly throne, and send down upon us, in return, the grace of your Holy Spirit.

When you entered within it, O Christ,
Salvation came to the house of Zaccheus.

Now let your holy angels enter among us
And bring this house your blessing.

Give us your peace, O Lord,
And your light and salvation to all who will live here.

PRAYER FOR BLESSING

*Make a large cross in the air with the incense or
by sprinkling the holy water as a blessing on the
house, and so on in each room.*

O Lord Jesus Christ, our God, when you entered into the house of Zaccheus the Tax Collector, you became his salvation and that of all his family. Grant to all who live here that they (we) may be protected from all that is evil. Bless them (us) and this house, O Lord, always preserving their (our) lives from all troubles, and granting to them (us) your abundant mercies: + For to you is due all glory, honor, and worship, with your Father who is without beginning, and your All-Holy, Good, and Life-Giving Spirit, now and ever and to the ages of ages. Amen.

In each room make the same sign of blessing, saying each time: "This room is blessed, sanctified, and protected, in the name of the Father, and of the Son, and of the Holy Spirit." Returning to the main room, hand out candles to the guests, if possible. When they are lighted, take up the book of the Gospels and read:

A READING FROM THE HOLY GOSPEL

Jesus entered Jericho and was passing through it. A man was there named Zaccheus; he was a senior tax collector and was rich. He tried hard to see who Jesus was, but the crowd was very great and he could not see anything at all because he was very short in stature. So he ran ahead and climbed a sycamore tree in order to get a better view, since he knew that Jesus had to pass by along that way. When Jesus came to the place, he looked up and said to him, "Zaccheus, hurry, come down; for I must stay at your house today." So he climbed down as fast as he could and was filled with joy that he could welcome him. All who saw this began to grumble and said, "Look. He has gone to be the guest of a sinful man." But Zaccheus stood his ground and said to the Lord, "Look, Lord, half of my possessions I will give to the poor; and if I have defrauded anyone in any way, I will pay back four times as much." Then Jesus said: "Today salvation has come to this house. For this man too is a son of Abraham. For the Son of Man came to seek out and to save what had been lost." (Lk. 19:1–10)

+ Glory to you, O Lord, glory to you.

LITANY OF INTERCESSION

In peace let us pray to the Lord.	Lord have mercy
For the church of God across the face of the earth	Lord have mercy
For all who live faithfully, seeking Christ's will	Lord have mercy
For the family who lives in this house	Lord have mercy
That Christ will always protect and bless them	Lord have mercy
For the suffering and the homeless	Lord have mercy
For captives and their salvation	Lord have mercy
For the oppressed and their deliverance	Lord have mercy
For the sick and the despairing	Lord have mercy
For those who have suffered loss or great sorrow	Lord have mercy
For our strengthening in joy and hope	Lord have mercy
For . . . *(the names and causes we wish to pray for)*	Lord have mercy
For all of us here who call on you from our hearts	Lord have mercy
	Lord have mercy
	Lord have mercy

FINAL PRAYER

Lord, send down your mercy and your blessing upon us here and upon this house. May your angel of mercy watch over it and keep all who live here safe from anything that is evil. May he guide us into the fulfillment of your holy will, teaching us to observe what Christ has taught us. O Lord, grant us health and length of days, giving us from your generous hand all that we need to live well and wisely. Save all those who are in want or trouble of any kind. May this house be known as a place of joy and mercy, where the kindness of Christ becomes real for all who live here and who visit. Be merciful to us, Lord: For you are a merciful God, who loves mankind, and to you we ascribe glory: + to the Father, and to the Son, and to the Holy Spirit, now and ever and to the ages of ages. Amen.

THE SEAL

+ Through the prayers of our holy Fathers and Mothers,
  Lord Jesus Christ our God, have mercy on us and save us. Amen.

Ritual for a Loved One Who Is Sick

Gather around the sick person. (If they are conscious, they need to be aware of the service and willing to participate in it—without necessarily having to take an active part.) Let the tone be one of quiet joy and hope in the Lord's mercy: dry all tears and freshen all faces, and trust entirely in God. Those attending may all carry lighted candles if it is judged safe to do so. Those praying seriously for the healing of another, in the times of the ancient church, used to fast and prepare themselves spiritually for this service by fervent prayer in the days preceding. Seriously consider, together with the sick person, the advisability of bringing an ordained minister into the house or hospital—who may be able to offer the sick person the church's sacraments of forgiveness, anointing, and Eucharist. These prayers of healing are not meant to substitute for the necessary seeking out of doctors and healers in our time of need. They are not mutually exclusive, as Scripture itself tells us: "Honor the physician with the appropriate honor, according to your need of him, for the Lord created the physician and all healing comes from the Most High" (Sir. 38:1).

THE OPENING BLESSING

+ In the name of the Father, and of the Son, and of the Holy Spirit. Amen.

Glory to you, our God, glory to you.

(or the "Seal")

THE TRISAGION PRAYERS
(repeat from pages 8–9)

INVITATORY PRAYER

+ Come let us worship and bow down before God our King.
  (bowing low each time)

+ Come let us worship and bow down before Christ, our King
  and God.

+ Come let us worship and bow down before Christ himself,
  our King and our God.

Psalm 70
(Alternate the Psalm text in two groups.)

In you, O Lord, I take refuge;
Let me never be put to shame.

In your justice rescue me, free me;
Pay heed to me and save me.

Be a rock where I can take refuge,
A mighty stronghold to save me;
For you are my rock, my stronghold.

Free me from the hand of the wicked,
From the grip of the unjust, of the oppressor.

It is you, O Lord, who are my hope,
My trust, O Lord, from my youth.

On you I have leaned from my birth;
From my mother's womb you have been my help.
My hope has always been in you.

My fate has filled many with awe
But you are my strong refuge.

My lips are filled with your praise,
With your glory all the day long.

Do not reject me now that I am old;
When my strength fails do not forsake me.

For my enemies are speaking about me;
Those who watch me take counsel together

Saying: "God has forsaken him; follow him,
Seize him; there is no one to save him."

O God, do not stay far off:
My God, make haste to help me!

Let them be put to shame and destroyed,
All those who seek my life.

Let them be covered with shame and confusion,
All those who seek to harm me.

But as for me, I will always hope
And praise you more and more.

My lips will tell of your justice
And day by day of your help
(Though I can never tell it all).

Lord, I will declare your mighty deeds
Proclaiming your justice, yours alone.

O God, you have taught me from my youth
And I proclaim your wonders still.

Now that I am old and gray-headed,
Do not forsake me, God.

Let me tell of your strength and justice to the skies,

Tell of you who have worked such wonders.
O God, who is like you?

You have burdened me with bitter troubles
But you will give me back my life.

You will raise me from the depths of the earth;
You will exalt me and console me again.

So I will give you thanks on the lyre
For your faithful love, O God.

To you will I sing with the harp,
To you, the Holy One of Israel.

When I sing to you my lips shall rejoice
And my soul, which you have redeemed.

And all the day long my tongue
Shall tell the tale of your justice:

For they are put to shame and disgraced,
All those who seek to harm me.

+ Glory to the Father, and to the Son, and to the Holy Spirit.
Now and ever and to the ages of ages. Amen.

+ Alleluia, Alleluia, Alleluia, glory to you, O God. *(three times)*

LITANY FOR THE SICK

(While one person reads the petitions, those present
respond, "Lord have mercy.")

In peace let us pray to the Lord.   Lord have mercy

For the peace from on high, and for the salvation
of our souls, let us pray to the Lord.   Lord have mercy

For the peace of the whole world, let us pray to
the Lord.   Lord have mercy

For this home and all who live here, let us pray
to the Lord.   Lord have mercy

For the servant of God –X– who is sick, that the
Lord may reconcile him *(her)* to himself, and show
him *(her)* great mercy, let us pray to the Lord.   Lord have mercy

That God may listen to our heartfelt prayer and
out of his compassionate love show mercy to his
servant, let us pray to the Lord.   Lord have mercy

As he once lifted up the paralyzed man from his bed
of illness, may he soon raise up the servant of God
–X– who now lies in illness, and grant him *(her)*
a return to health; let us ask of the Lord.   Lord have mercy

That he will grant his servant –X– the gift of his
Holy Spirit, to heal him *(her)* of every infirmity
of soul and body, let us ask of the Lord.   Lord have mercy

As he once listened to the crying of the Canaanite
woman, may he hear us now. As he was once merciful
to her daughter, may he show us his compassion
now and heal his servant –X– who is sick,
let us ask the Lord.   Lord have mercy

Help us, save us, have mercy on us, and keep us,
O God, by your grace.   Lord have mercy

Calling to mind our Most Holy, Immaculate,
Most Blessed and Glorious Lady, the Mother of God
and Ever-Virgin Mary, with all the saints, let us
commend ourselves, and each other, and all our life,
to Christ our God.

                                              Lord have mercy

For you, O God, are merciful and full of compassion and to you we ascribe
glory:

  + To the Father, and to the Son, and to the Holy Spirit.
     Now and ever and to the ages of ages. Amen.

A READING FROM THE LETTER OF ST. JAMES

Dear ones, do not grumble against one another, and you will be spared
judgment. See, the Judge is already standing at the doors! As an example
of suffering and patience, dear ones, take the prophets who spoke in the
name of the Lord. How rightly are those who showed endurance called
blessed. You must have heard of the endurance of Job, and you have seen
the purpose of the Lord, how the Lord is compassionate and merciful.
Above all, my dear ones, do not swear, either by heaven or by earth or by
any other oath, but let your word be a simple yes for yes, and no for no,
so that you may not fall under condemnation. Are there any among you
who are suffering? They should pray. Are there any filled with good heart?
They should sing songs of praise. Are there any among you who have fallen
sick? They should call for the elders of the church and have them pray over
them, anointing them with oil in the name of the Lord. Because the prayer
of faith will save the person who is sick, and the Lord will raise them up;
and if anyone has committed sins, these will be forgiven also. Therefore,
confess your sins to one another, and pray for one another, so that you may

find healing. The prayer of righteous people is both powerful and effective. (Jas. 5:9–16)

+ Alleluia, Alleluia, Alleluia, glory to you, O God.

A READING FROM THE HOLY GOSPEL

When Jesus had come down from the mountain, great crowds followed him; and there was a leper who came up to him and knelt before him, saying, "Lord, if you want to, you can make me clean." Jesus stretched out his hand and touched him, saying, "I do want to. Be made clean!" Immediately his leprosy was cleansed. Then Jesus said to him, "See that you say nothing about this to anyone; but go, show yourself to the priest, and offer the gift that Moses commanded, as a testimony to them." Jesus then entered Capernaum, and a centurion came up to him, making an appeal to him, saying, "Lord, my servant is lying at home paralyzed, in terrible distress." And Jesus said to him, "I will come and heal him." The centurion made this reply, "Lord, I am not worthy to have you come under my roof; only speak the word, and my servant will be healed. For I also am a man under authority, with soldiers under me; and I say to one, 'Go,' and he goes, and I say to another, 'Come,' and he comes, and I say to my slave, 'Do this,' and he must do it." When Jesus heard him, he was amazed and said to his followers, "I tell you solemnly, I have not found such faith in anyone in Israel. I tell you this: many will come from east and west and will eat with Abraham and Isaac and Jacob in the kingdom of heaven, while the heirs of the kingdom will be cast into the dimness of the margins, where there will be weeping and gnashing of teeth." And turning to the centurion, Jesus said, "Go home; It will be done for you according as you have believed." And the man's servant was healed in that very hour. Now when Jesus entered into the house of Peter, he saw his mother-in-law lying in bed with a fever; he touched her hand, and the fever left her, and she got up and began to serve him. That evening they brought to him many who were possessed with demons; and he cast out the spirits with a word, and he cured all who were sick. This was to fulfill what had been foretold through the prophet Isaiah, "He took our infirmities upon himself, and bore our diseases." (Matt. 8:1–17)

+ Alleluia, Alleluia, Alleluia, glory to you, O God. *(three times)*

PRAYER FOR HEALING

All those present now pray fervently and silently for the gift of the Spirit of God on the sick person. The leader of the service should place their confidence in the mercy of God, the Giver of Our Life and only source of the grace of healing, and with faith and trust offer this prayer over the sick person, who, if possible, holds the cross or the book of the Gospels while it is being said, themselves calling on the Spirit of God.

Almighty Master, Holy King and Physician of our souls, you correct us so that we do not go wholly astray, and when we fall you raise us up again. When we are cast down, you lift us up once more. You heal the afflictions of our human race, which you love with a Father's care. We pray to you, our gracious God, that in your mercy you would visit the servant of God –X–, who is sick, and grant him *(her)* healing of body and soul. Send down from on high your healing power. Touch the body, quench the fever, soothe the sorrow, relieve the suffering, and cast out every hidden malady from within. Be the Good Physician of your servant –X– and raise him *(her)* up from this bed of affliction to the full perfection of health, granting to him *(her)*, through the ministry of your church, your good will and your favor.

If possible, the leader of the service here will gently lay his or her hand upon the sick person's head and use their thumb to sign their forehead with the sign of the cross, saying:

And so, give to your servant –X– the grace of your healing. + In the name of the Father, and of the Son, and of the Holy Spirit. For you are a God of mercy and compassion, and to you we ascribe glory: to the Father, and to the Son, and to the Holy Spirit, now and ever and to the ages of ages. Amen.

CONCLUDING PRAYERS

Glory to you, O Christ, our God and our hope. Glory to you.

Lord have mercy   Lord have mercy   Lord have mercy

Look down on the prayers of your servants, Immaculate Mother of God, and help us in our distress. You are our constant advocate and protector. Open to us the gates of your compassion, and free us from our sorrows, O Sovereign Lady, that we may not be put to shame in our prayers. We cry out to you in faith: "In you all creation rejoices."

+ Through the prayer of our holy Fathers and Mothers,
     Lord Jesus Christ our God, have mercy on us and save us. Amen.

Additional Prayers for the Sick

BEFORE AN OPERATION

Lord Jesus Christ, who patiently endured all your sufferings, even the scourging and laceration of your most holy body, so that you might save the souls and bodies of all our race, look kindly now upon the suffering body of your servant –X– and give him *(her)* the strength with patience and courage to endure the trials, whatever they may be, that you have permitted to fall upon him *(her)*. Give your blessing to the hands that will work toward his *(her)* healing, working through their skill to perfect your servant's salvation in both body and soul. For you are a merciful God, and you wish to show us mercy and save us, O Christ our God, and to you we ascribe glory, + together with your eternal Father, and your All-Holy, Good, and Life-Giving Spirit, now and ever and to the ages of ages. Amen.

FOR A SICK CHILD

Lord Jesus Christ, who came into this world as a little child, and even as divine Lord were subject to your parents, look down now upon your child –X– who lies in sickness. You entered into the room of the little daughter of Jairus and his wife, and called out to the child: "My Little Lamb, get up again," and she rose back to life and health. Now call out to the servant of God, the child –X– who has been brought low by illness and needs your assistance. Strengthen him *(her)* in body and soul. Give him *(her)* cheerfulness and courage and endurance to support all the trials that you have permitted to fall upon him *(her)*. Stretch out your holy right hand over him *(her)* so that being restored to the full vigor of health he *(she)* may reach maturity of years and serve you gratefully and faithfully all the days of his *(her)* life. For you are the Good Physician of our souls and bodies,

Christ our God, and to you we ascribe glory, + to the Father, and to the Son, and to the Holy Spirit, now and ever and to the ages of ages. Amen.

WHEN SICKNESS INCREASES

O Lord Jesus Christ our Savior, for our sake you accepted all things: were born into this world, went hungry and thirsty, suffered violence, and gave your life over to the power of death. Now you have allowed your servant —X— to know some share in your sufferings. So too allow him *(her)* to know the mercy of your grace and presence. May your precious body and blood cleanse and deliver him *(her)* , strengthen and encourage him *(her)* . May your own holiness be his *(her)* righteousness and reconciliation. When they come to stand before your throne, do not look upon his *(her)* works, but look instead on his *(her)* faith in you and his *(her)* love. As his *(her)* sickness increases in severity, so also let your wondrous grace increase within him *(her)* . Do not allow his *(her)* faith to waver because of his *(her)* grief and trouble, and do not allow his *(her)* hope to grow dim or his *(her)* love to grow cold. Do not allow the fearfulness of death to grip his *(her)* heart or turn aside his *(her)* trust in you, or cause him *(her)* to place that trust anywhere else except in you. Help him *(her)* to look into your face with unblinking eye to the very end of life on this earth, and then let him *(her)* say in all hopefulness: "Lord, into your hands I commend my spirit," as you yourself prayed on the cross; for in this way he *(she)* shall enter joyfully into your everlasting kingdom, + of the Father, and of the Son, and of the Holy Spirit, now and ever and to the ages of ages. Amen.

FOR THOSE SUFFERING MENTAL ANGUISH

Lord Jesus Christ, our God who is full of mercy and compassion and love for our race, when you were faced with the dark hostility of men, your heart was filled with grief and overcome with suffering in the Garden of Gethsemane. Your mental pain was then so great that drops of blood fell down from your troubled brow. Look down now upon your servant –X– who struggles with the griefs and sorrows of the mind, who is cast down and filled with anxiety because of so many trials. Give him *(her)* your own peace, your own courage. Make him *(her)* know that you are beside him *(her)* as their comfort and strength. Stretch out your right hand to lift him *(her)* up and save him *(her)* in both body and soul; for you are a good and most loving God, + and to you we ascribe all glory, along with your Everlasting Father, and your All-Holy Spirit, now and ever and to the ages of ages. Amen.

AFTER A FAILED SUICIDE ATTEMPT

Almighty God, Creator and Redeemer of all humanity, it was you who gave us the gift of life in this world, so that we may be prepared for the life to come after serving you in faithfulness and courage all the days of our life. It is you who help us in times of trouble and distress, raising us up when we fall down. It is you, O God, who have prevented your suffering servant –X– who has been so cast down by sorrow that he *(she)* has tried, unsuccessfully, to end his *(her)* life on this earth, forgetting his *(her)* immortal destiny promised by you, to be in the joy and company of the saints and angels in the radiance of your resurrection. Lord, forgive your poor servant who has suffered from the malice and evil that surrounds him *(her)* on all sides. Lift him *(her)* up once more, restore him *(her)* by your grace, and let him *(her)* weep healing tears and by them to be reconciled to your love. For you are the sure and steadfast God of all who turn to you with a broken and needy heart: + and to you we ascribe glory, to the Father, and to the Son, and to the Holy Spirit, now and ever and to the ages of ages. Amen.

Prayer Service for a Sick Animal

God loves all his creatures, and those we care about deeply, or on whom we rely for our welfare, are themselves closely bound up with us in "walking the ways of salvation." The ancient church has used a similar prayer service for centuries. If the animal has a name, use it in the text. If there is holy water in the house, use this in one of the prayers of blessing (below) or say a prayer of blessing over incense (see the earlier ritual for a house blessing), and this may also be used to make the form of a cross over the creature.

Begin the service facing east in the presence of the sick animal, but not crowding it.

THE OPENING BLESSING

+ Blessed is our God, + always now and ever and to the ages of ages. Amen.

Glory to you, our God, glory to you.

(or the "Seal")

THE TRISAGION PRAYERS
(repeat from pages 8–9)

INVITATORY PRAYER

+ Come let us worship and bow down before God our King.
(bowing low each time)
+ Come let us worship and bow down before Christ, our King and God.
+ Come let us worship and bow down before Christ himself, our King and our God.

Psalm 68

(vv. 2–4, 14–18, 31–35)

Save me, O God,
For the waters have risen to my neck.

I have sunk into the mud of the deep
And there is no foothold.

I have entered the waters of the deep
And the waves overwhelm me.

I am wearied with all my crying,
My throat is parched.

My eyes are wasted away
From looking for my God.

This is my prayer to you,
My prayer for your favor.

In your great love, answer me, O God,
With your help that never fails;

Rescue me from sinking in the mud,
Save me from my foes.

Save me from the waters of the deep
Lest the waves overwhelm me.

Do not let the deep engulf me
Nor death close its mouth on me.

Lord, answer, for your love is kind;
In your compassion, turn towards me.

Do not hide your face from your servant;
Answer me quickly for I am in distress.

I will praise God's name with a song;
I will glorify him with thanksgiving.

A gift pleasing God more than oxen,
More than beasts prepared for sacrifice.

The poor when they see it will be glad
And God-seeking hearts will revive;

For the Lord listens to the needy
And does not spurn his servants in their troubles.

Let the heavens and the earth give him praise,
The sea and all its living creatures.

> + Glory to the Father, and to the Son, and to the Holy Spirit.
>   Now and ever and to the ages of ages. Amen.

> + Alleluia, Alleluia, Alleluia, Glory to you, O God. *(three times)*

PRAYER OF BLESSING

Lord Jesus Christ, our God, you are strong and majestic, and carry in your hand the power of life and death. You alone are the salvation of both humans and beasts. Hear us graciously who call upon you in this time of need, for we bow down before you with humility and in sorrow of heart. In your time on earth you were sheltered by ox and donkey, you rode into Jerusalem on a young foal, and told your disciples that the birds of the air were protected by your Father's holy providence. Look down now upon this sick creature that has been brought low because of its infirmities. By the power of your life-giving blessing, heal it and calm its sickness. Drive away from it all that is evil and restore it to health. We ask your mercy through the prayers of your Most Holy Mother, the Ever-Virgin Mary, by the power of your holy cross . . .

+ *Make the sign of the cross over the sick animal, and gently lay your hands upon it if possible.* +

. . . through the prayers of your saints who through the ages have delighted in mediating your grace of healing to the church: saints Cosmas and Damian, Cyrus and John, Panteleimon and all your saints. For you are the Giver of our Life, and you are the salvation of both humans and beasts, and to you we ascribe glory: + to the Father, and to the Son, and to the Holy Spirit, now and ever and to the ages of ages. Amen.

Psalm 66

O God, be gracious and bless us
And let your face shed its light upon us.

So will your ways be known upon earth
And all nations learn your saving help.

Let the peoples praise you, O God;
Let all the peoples praise you.

Let the nations be glad and exult
For you rule the world with justice.

With fairness you rule the peoples,
You guide the nations on earth.

Let the peoples praise you, O God;
Let all the peoples praise you.

The earth has yielded its fruit
For God, our God, has blessed us.

May God still give us his blessing
Till the ends of the earth revere him.

+ Alleluia, Alleluia, Alleluia, glory to you, O God. *(three times)*

If there is holy water in the house, place some on your fingers and gently put it over the animal in the form of a cross. Or, if you have incense, say over it a prayer of blessing: "Incense we offer you, O Christ our God. Accept it at your heavenly throne, and send down upon us, in return, the grace of your Holy Spirit," and make a sign of the cross in the air above and over the sick animal, saying this prayer of blessing:

SECOND PRAYER OF BLESSING

O Lord, may all sickness and infirmity be extinguished and driven away from this suffering creature. May all evil and malady flee from it by the power of your holy cross: + in the name of the Father, and of the Son, and of the Holy Spirit. Amen.

FINAL PRAYER TO THE MOTHER OF GOD

Look down on the prayers of your servants, Immaculate Mother of God, and help us in our distress. You are our constant advocate and protector. Open to us the gates of your compassion, and free us from our sorrows, O Sovereign Lady, that we may not be put to shame in our prayers. We cry out to you in faith: "In you all creation rejoices."

THE SEAL

+ Through the prayers of our holy Fathers and Mothers,
Lord Jesus Christ our God, have mercy on us and save us. Amen.

Prayers for a Home Troubled by an Evil Atmosphere

God is our loving Father and the presence of his grace inevitably and irresistibly casts out all evil, just as the dawning light of a new day dispels the gloom of the night. The darkness cannot resist the light but will always flee from its presence. The ancient saints used to say that the presence of the good was recognized because of its accompanying peacefulness and joy. Conversely, the presence of evil and malice could be recognized because of the way it fosters agitation, bitterness, and a sense of oppression. Today many may feel a sense of oppression and anxiety in their homes and do not know where to turn. To arrange a blessing of the home by an ordained minister is a good start. One should permanently set up a cross in the house, as no evil thing can withstand the cross of Christ. The following is a short service of prayer for those who feel oppressed by a place, or oppressed by evil in themselves. In the longer term, the best of all liberations is to seek the sacraments of reconciliation and Eucharist in a supportive Christian community.

First set up a cross, and light a candle before it.

THE OPENING BLESSING

+ In the name of the Father, and of the Son, and of the Holy Spirit. Amen.

Glory to you, our God, glory to you.

(or the "Seal")

THE TRISAGION PRAYERS
(repeat from pages 8–9)

INVITATORY PRAYER

+ Come let us worship and bow down before God our King.
   (bowing low each time)

+ Come let us worship and bow down before Christ, our King
   and God.

+ Come let us worship and bow down before Christ himself,
   our King and our God.

Psalm 90

One who dwells in the shelter of the Most High
And abides in the shade of the Almighty

Says to the Lord: "My refuge,
My stronghold, my God in whom I trust!"

It is he who will free you from the snare of the fowler
Who seeks to destroy you;

He will conceal you with his pinions
And under his wings you will find refuge.

You will not fear the terror of the night
Nor the arrow that flies by day,

Nor the plague that prowls in the darkness
Nor the scourge that lays waste at noon.

A thousand may fall at your side,
Ten thousand fall at your right,

You, it will never approach;
His faithfulness is buckler and shield.

Your eyes have only to look
To see how the wicked are repaid,

You who have said: "Lord, my refuge!"
And have made the Most High your dwelling.

Upon you no evil shall fall,
No plague approach where you dwell.

For you has he commanded his angels,
To keep you in all your ways.

They shall bear you upon their hands
Lest you strike your foot against a stone.

On the lion and the viper you will tread
And trample the young lion and the dragon.

One who clings to me in love, I will set free;
Protect the one who knows my name.

Call out and I shall answer: "I am with you."
I will save you in distress and give you glory.

With length of life I will content you.
I shall let you see my saving power.

> + Glory to the Father, and to the Son, and to the Holy Spirit.
> Now and ever and to the ages of ages. Amen.

> + Alleluia, Alleluia, Alleluia, glory to you, O Lord. *(three times)*

Psalm 115

I trusted, even when I said:
"I am sorely afflicted,"

And when I said in my alarm:
"No man can be trusted."

How can I repay the Lord
For his goodness to me?

The cup of salvation I will raise;
I will call on the Lord's name.

My vows to the Lord I will fulfill
Before all his people.

O precious in the eyes of the Lord
Is the death of his faithful.

Your servant, Lord, your servant am I;
You have loosened my bonds.

A thanksgiving sacrifice I make;
I will call on the Lord's name.

My vows to the Lord I will fulfill
Before all his people,

In the courts of the house of the Lord,
In your midst, O Jerusalem.

Psalm 96

The Lord is king, let earth rejoice,
Let all the coastlands be glad.

Cloud and darkness are his raiment;
His throne, justice and right.

A fire prepares his path;
It burns up his foes on every side.

His lightnings light up the world,
The earth trembles at the sight.

The mountains melt like wax
Before the Lord of all the earth.

The skies proclaim his justice;
All peoples see his glory.

Let those who serve idols be ashamed,
Those who boast of their worthless gods.
All you spirits, worship him.

Zion hears and is glad;
The people of Judah rejoice
Because of your judgments, O Lord.

For you indeed are the Lord
Most high above all the earth,
Exalted far above all spirits.

The Lord loves those who hate evil;
He guards the souls of his saints;
He sets them free from the wicked.

Light shines forth for the just
And joy for the upright of heart.

Rejoice, you just, in the Lord;
Give glory to his holy name.

+ Glory to the Father, and to the Son, and to the Holy Spirit.
Now and ever and to the ages of ages. Amen.

+ Alleluia, Alleluia, Alleluia, glory to you, O Lord. *(three times)*

LITANY OF INTERCESSION

In peace let us pray to the Lord.	Lord have mercy
For the church of God across the face of the earth	Lord have mercy
For all who live faithfully, seeking Christ's will	Lord have mercy
For the suffering and the homeless	Lord have mercy
For captives and their salvation	Lord have mercy
For the oppressed and their deliverance	Lord have mercy
For the sick and the despairing	Lord have mercy
For those who have suffered loss or great sorrow	Lord have mercy
For our strengthening in joy and hope	Lord have mercy
For . . . *(the names and causes we wish to pray for)*	Lord have mercy
For all of us who call on you from our hearts	Lord have mercy
	Lord have mercy
	Lord have mercy

PRAYER OF ST. BASIL FOR DELIVERANCE FROM EVIL OPPRESSION

O God of Gods and Lord of Lords, Creator of the fiery angels and Maker of the bodiless powers, you are the Lord of all things in heaven, on earth, and under the earth. No human eye is able to look upon you. All creation stands in existence only because of your grace. The evil archangel was cast down from heaven because of his pride and disobedience, and brought down with him many of the angels, so that they turned into evil demons. Let your Holy Name, O God, be among us now, let it cast out all manner of evil from this house, and all malign influence. Let your Holy Name, O God, be terrible to the powers of evil and banish them from this place so that no harm may come to those who live here, your disciples who are made in your holy image.

O Lord Jesus Christ, you said to your apostles: "See, I have given you the power to trample on serpents and scorpions, and all the power of the Enemy." By your cross you cast down the powers of evil and led Satan captive because of your holy incarnation. You are the hope of all who place their trust in you, and a strong defense for all who rely on you. By this holy sign . . . +

(Those present make the sign of the cross over themselves.)

. . . drive away from this dwelling all manner of evil. Preserve all who live in this house from harm and from all faithlessness. Let your holy angels teach them the psalm: "The Lord is my Help, I shall not be afraid. I will fear no evil because you are with me." Deliver us and save us O Lord, our loving and merciful God: + for yours is the kingdom and the power and the glory: of the Father, and of the Son, and of the Holy Spirit, now and ever and to the ages of ages. Amen.

FINAL PRAYER AND BLESSING

Look down on the prayers of your servants, Immaculate Mother of God, and help us in our distress. You are our constant advocate and protector. Open to us the gates of your compassion, and free us from our sorrows, O Sovereign Lady, that we may not be put to shame in our prayers. We cry out to you in faith: "In you all creation rejoices."

+ Through the prayers of our holy Fathers and Mothers,
   Lord Jesus Christ our God, have mercy on us and save us. Amen.

Ritual on the Occasion of a Death

If a person is close to death, the book of Psalms can be read slowly, gently, and quietly in the room.

Psalms 23 (The Lord is my Shepherd), 90 (One who dwells in the shelter of the Most High), 129, 89, 120, 22, and 102 LXX are particularly appropriate to begin.

It is a time when a family may wish to call in an ordained minister who may offer the dying person counsel, consolation, and the sacraments of the church.

This service is useful for a domestic occasion, when the family has gathered. At the time of death, it is a good thing to read also the Passion account of the Gospel of St. John: especially John 19:17–30.

After death and when the dead person has been laid out (or when the family can gather at the funeral parlor), stand or kneel around the body with lighted candles.

THE OPENING BLESSING

+ Blessed is our God, + always now and ever and to the ages of ages. Amen.

Glory to you, our God, glory to you.

(or the "Seal")

THE TRISAGION PRAYERS
(repeat from pages 8–9)

INVITATORY PRAYER

+ Come let us worship and bow down before God our King.
  (bowing low each time)
+ Come let us worship and bow down before Christ, our King and God.
+ Come let us worship and bow down before Christ himself, our King and our God.

Psalm 129

Out of the depths I cry to you, O Lord,
Lord, hear my voice!

O let your ears be attentive
To the voice of my pleading.

If you, O Lord, should mark our guilt,
Lord, who would survive?

But with you is found forgiveness:
For this we revere you.

My soul is waiting for the Lord.
I count on his word.

My soul is longing for the Lord
More than watchman for daybreak.

Let the watchman count on daybreak
And Israel on the Lord.

Because with the Lord there is mercy
And fullness of redemption,

Israel indeed he will redeem
From all its iniquity.

Psalm 120

I lift up my eyes to the mountains;
From where shall come my help?

My help shall come from the Lord
Who made heaven and earth.

May he never allow you to stumble!
May your guard never sleep.

No, he sleeps not nor slumbers,
Israel's guard.

The Lord is your guard and your shade;
At your right side he stands.

By day the sun shall not smite you
Nor the moon in the night.

The Lord will guard you from evil;
He will guard your soul.

The Lord will guard your going and coming
Both now and for ever.

Psalm 102

My soul, give thanks to the Lord.
All my being, bless his holy name.

My soul, give thanks to the Lord
And never forget all his blessings.

It is he who forgives all your guilt,
Who heals every one of your ills,

Who redeems your life from the grave,
Who crowns you with love and compassion,

Who fills your life with good things,
Renewing your youth like an eagle's.

The Lord does deeds of justice,
Gives judgment for all who are oppressed.

He made known his ways to Moses
And his deeds to all Israel.

The Lord is compassion and love,
Slow to anger and rich in mercy.

His wrath will come to an end;
He will not be angry for ever.

He does not treat us according to our sins,
Nor repay us according to our faults.

For as the heavens are high above the earth
So strong is his love for those who fear him.

As far as the east is from the west,
So far does he remove our sins.

As a father has compassion on his child,
The Lord has pity on those who fear him;

For he knows of what we are made,
He remembers that we are dust.

For humans, the days are like grass;
We flower like the flower of the field;

The wind blows and we are gone
And our place never sees us again.

But the love of the Lord is everlasting
Upon those who hold him in fear;

His justice reaches out to children's children
When they keep his covenant in truth,

When they keep his will in their mind.
The Lord has set his sway in heaven

And his kingdom is ruling over all.
Give thanks to the Lord, all his angels,

Mighty in power, fulfilling his word,
Who heed the voice of his word.

Give thanks to the Lord, all his hosts,
His servants who do his will.

Give thanks to the Lord, all his works,
In every place where he rules.
My soul, give thanks to the Lord!

+ Glory to the Father, and to the Son, and to the Holy Spirit.
   Now and ever and to the ages of ages. Amen.

+ Alleluia, Alleluia, Alleluia, glory to you, O Lord. *(three times)*

PRAYERS FOR THE DEPARTED

We, who have long known that death would come to us,
Are faced with it now, Blessed Mother of God.
Weeping, we cry out to you: do not forget us in our hour of need.
Intercede for us in our distress and reach out your hand
To your servant –X–, who has departed this life.

Lord Jesus Christ, illumine with your divine light
The soul of this your servant –X–,
Who has woken up to you in a new dawn of love.
Grant that he *(she)* may recognize you, Word of God, the true God,
Who calls him *(her)* out of the gloom of this deceptive life.

Lord Almighty, the Father of Our Lord Jesus Christ, it is your will that all human beings should be saved and come to the knowledge of the truth. You have said that you do not desire the death of a sinner, but rather that we should turn and live again. We pray to you now to forgive your servant –X–, who has departed this life, every transgression that he *(she)* may have committed; for you are the One who can resolve all things that are impossible for us. You are the hope of those who despair, the strong support of all who put their trust in you. Lord, receive in peace the soul of this your servant –X– and grant them rest in the dwelling places of heaven, in the company of the saints. + We ask this through the grace of your Only Begotten Son, our Lord and God and Savior Jesus Christ: with whom you are blessed, together with your All-Holy, Good, and Life-Giving Spirit; now and ever and to the ages of ages. Amen.

Lord, give peace now to your servant –X–, who has departed this life, and grant him *(her)* rest where the souls of the righteous dwell, in a place of light and green pasture; a place from which every sorrow and sighing has been banished; a place where the light of your face falls on them to comfort them. For you, O Lord, are the repose of our souls and bodies, and to you we give glory: + to the Father, and to the Son, and to the Holy Spirit. Now and ever and to the ages of ages. Amen.

A READING FROM THE HOLY SCRIPTURE

Brothers and sisters, I do not want you to be in confusion about the state of those who have died, and then you will not grieve as others do who have no hope. For since we believe that Jesus died and rose again, even so, through Jesus, God will bring those who have died to himself. For I tell you solemnly, by the word of the Lord, that we who are alive, and who are left until the coming of the Lord, will by no means have an advantage over those who have died. For the Lord himself, with a shout of command, and with the archangel's mighty call, and with the sound of God's trumpet, will descend from heaven, and the dead in Christ will be the first to rise. Then afterward, we who are left here still alive, will be caught up in the clouds together with them to meet the Lord in the air. In this way all of us shall be with the Lord forever. Accordingly, give heart to one another with these words. (1 Thess. 4:13–18)

LITANY OF INTERCESSION

In peace let us pray to the Lord.	Lord have mercy
For the church of God across the face of the earth	Lord have mercy
For all who live faithfully, seeking Christ's will	Lord have mercy
For the suffering and the homeless	Lord have mercy
For captives and their salvation	Lord have mercy
For the oppressed and their deliverance	Lord have mercy
For the sick and the despairing	Lord have mercy
For those who have suffered loss or great sorrow	Lord have mercy
For our strengthening in joy and hope	Lord have mercy
For . . . *(the names and causes we wish to pray for)*	Lord have mercy
For all of us who call on you from our hearts	Lord have mercy
	Lord have mercy
	Lord have mercy

PRAYER OF INTERCESSION

Christ our true God, you have dominion over the living and the dead. Through the prayers of your All-Holy Mother, and of all the saints, establish the soul of your servant –X– in the company of the blessed, and have mercy upon us who grieve and are filled with sorrow. You alone are the Immortal One, who made us and fashioned us. But we were made of dust, and to the dust we shall return, according to your commandment. Even so, as we poor mortals make our way, we lift up this song as our funeral chant: Alleluia, Alleluia, Alleluia. You are our God who descended into the depths of hell and there untied the bonds of its captives. Now give rest to the soul of your departed servant –X–: + for you are a kind and gracious

God who loves humankind, and to you we offer praise and thanksgiving, with your All-Holy, Good, and Life-Giving Spirit, in the glory of God the Father. Amen.

THE SEAL

+ Through the prayers of our holy Fathers and Mothers,
  Lord Jesus Christ our God, have mercy on us and save us. Amen.

Prayers in Time of Sorrow

THE OPENING BLESSING

+ In the name of the Father, and of the Son, and of the Holy Spirit. Amen.

Glory to you, our God, glory to you.

(or the "Seal")

THE TRISAGION PRAYERS
(repeat from pages 8–9)

INVITATORY PRAYER

+ Come let us worship and bow down before God our King.
(bowing low each time)
+ Come let us worship and bow down before Christ, our King and God.
+ Come let us worship and bow down before Christ himself, our King and our God.

Psalm 87

Lord my God, I call for help by day;
I cry at night before you.

Let my prayer come into your presence.
O turn your ear to my cry.

For my soul is filled with evils;
My life is on the brink of the grave.

I am reckoned as one in the tomb:
I have reached the end of my strength,

Like one alone among the dead,
Like the slain lying in their graves,

Like those you remember no more,
Cut off, as they are, from your hand.

You have laid me in the depths of the tomb,
In places that are dark, in the depths.

Your anger weighs down upon me;
I am drowned beneath your waves.

You have taken away my friends
And made me hateful in their sight.

Imprisoned, I cannot escape;
My eyes are sunken with grief.

I call to you, Lord, all the day long;
To you I stretch out my hands.

Will you work your wonders for the dead?
Will the shades stand and praise you?

Will your love be told in the grave
Or your faithfulness among the dead?

Will your wonders be known in the dark
Or your justice in the land of oblivion?

As for me, Lord, I call to you for help;
In the morning my prayer comes before you.

Lord, why do you reject me?
Why do you hide your face?

Wretched, close to death from my youth,
I have borne your trials; I am numb.

Your fury has swept down upon me;
your terrors have utterly destroyed me.

They surround me all the day like a flood,
They assail me all together.

Friend and neighbor you have taken away:
My one companion is darkness.

Psalm 33

(vv. 2–8, 16–21, 23)

I will bless the Lord at all times,
His praise always on my lips;

In the Lord my soul shall make its boast.
The humble shall hear and be glad.

Glorify the Lord with me.
Together let us praise his name.

I sought the Lord and he answered me;
From all my terrors he set me free.

Look towards him and be radiant;
Let your faces not be cast down.

This poor one called, and the Lord heard
And rescued me from all my distress.

The angel of the Lord is encamped
Around those who revere him, to rescue them.

The Lord turns his face against the wicked
To destroy their remembrance from the earth.

The Lord turns his eyes to the just
And his ears to their appeal.

They call and the Lord hears
And rescues them in all their distress.

The Lord is close to the broken-hearted;
Those whose spirit is crushed he will save.

Many are the trials of the just one
But from them all the Lord will rescue him.

He will keep guard over all his bones,
Not one of his bones shall be broken.

The Lord ransoms the souls of his servants.
Those who hide in him shall not be condemned.

Psalm 85

Turn your ear, O Lord, and give answer
for I am poor and needy.

Preserve my life, for I am faithful;
Save the servant who trusts in you.

You are my God, have mercy on me, Lord,
For I cry to you all the day long.

Give joy to your servant, O Lord,
For to you I lift up my soul.

O Lord, you are good and forgiving,
Full of love to all who call.

Give heed, O Lord, to my prayer
And attend to the sound of my voice.

In the day of distress I will call
and surely you will reply.

Among the gods there is none like you, O Lord;
Nor work to compare with yours.

All the nations shall come to adore you
And glorify your name, O Lord:

For you are great and do marvelous deeds,
You who alone are God.

Show me, Lord, your way
So that I may walk in your truth.
Guide my heart to fear your name.

I will praise you, Lord my God, with all my heart
And glorify your name for ever;

For your love to me has been great:
you have saved me from the depths of the grave.

The proud have risen against me;
Ruthless men seek my life;
To you they pay no heed.

But you, God of mercy and compassion,
Slow to anger, O Lord,

Abounding in love and truth,
Turn and take pity on me.

O give your strength to your servant
And save your handmaid's child.

Show me the sign of your favor
That my foes may see to their shame
That you console me and give me your help.

> + Glory to the Father, and to the Son, and to the Holy Spirit.
> Now and ever and to the ages of ages. Amen.

> + Alleluia, Alleluia, Alleluia, glory to you, O Lord. *(three times)*

PRAYER FOR GOD'S FAVOR

O Lord, I bear your holy image in the depths of my soul, and though
marred by faults, it is still radiant with your own ineffable glory. I cry out
to you from the depths, cast down into despondency. Of old you made me
from the dust of the earth, and often to the dust I fall. But restore to me
that radiance of your image and lift me again to my ancient beauty. Show
your compassion to your creature, Lord, and raise me up once more to be
able to sing to you in praise with a glad and lightened heart, with renewed
vigor and hope: + for you are a God of mercy and compassion, and to you
we offer glory: to the Father, and to the Son, and to the Holy Spirit. Now
and ever and to the ages of ages. Amen.

READING FROM THE HOLY GOSPEL

And Jesus said to them: But now I am returning to him who sent me. Yet
none of you asks me, where is it you are going? But because I have said

these things, sorrow has filled your hearts. Even so, I tell you the truth: it is to your advantage that I should depart, for if I do not depart, the Paraclete will not come to you. But if I do go, I will send him to you. And when he comes, he will convince the world concerning sin and righteousness and judgment. I still have so many things to tell you, but you cannot bear them now. When the Spirit of Truth comes, he will guide you into all the truth. Truly, truly, I say to you, you will weep and lament, while the world rejoices. You will be full of sorrow: but your sorrow will turn into joy. When a woman is in labor she has much sorrow, because her hour has come; but when she has given birth to the child, she can no longer remember the anguish, because of the joy that a child is newly born into the world. So it is with you: you have sorrow now, but I will see you again and your hearts will rejoice. And then no one will take your joy from you. (Jn. 16:5–8, 12–13, 20–22)

PRAYER OF INTERCESSION

O Lord, once the blind man called out to you repeatedly on the Jericho road: "Jesus, Son of David, have pity on me." And the mother of the Syrophoenician girl who was oppressed by evil never ceased following you and crying out: "Lord, be my help." When the mother-in-law of Peter lay sick, you touched her hand and raised her up. Your apostle taught us that in the days of your flesh even you yourself prayed to the Father with sighs and tears that he might deliver you. Despondency of heart and soul has overwhelmed us, Lord. We are cast about like little ships on the sea of the troubles and sorrows of this life. We call to you, our constant hope and strong defense: be a Savior to us who are brought low and strengthen us once more by your presence and your grace. Calm the troubled seas as once you brought hope and consolation to your disciples, paralyzed by fear upon the Sea of Galilee. Give us courage and renew the springs of joy

in our heart that we live and praise you in gladness and freedom of soul:
+ for you are a loving and merciful God, and to you we give glory: to the
Father, and to the Son, and to the Holy Spirit. Now and ever and to the
ages of ages. Amen.

LITANY OF INTERCESSION

Let us pray for the peace of the world:	Lord have mercy
And for all the church of Christ across the face of the earth	Lord have mercy
For our leaders and mentors, and all who help and encourage us	Lord have mercy
For those who love us, and for those who hate us	Lord have mercy
For those in danger and distress	Lord have mercy
For all those who have asked for our prayers	Lord have mercy
For travelers by land and sea and air	Lord have mercy
For all who lie in sickness	Lord have mercy
For the flourishing of the harvests of the earth	Lord have mercy
For . . . *(special needs may be mentioned)*	Lord have mercy
For our parents and teachers who have departed this life	Lord have mercy
And for all Christ's faithful who lie asleep in the Lord	Lord have mercy
And for ourselves we say	Lord have mercy
	Lord have mercy
	Lord have mercy

PRAYER TO THE MOTHER OF GOD

In you, O Virgin Mother of God, we have a Wall of Defense and a
    Refuge,
An Intercessor pleasing to God, whom you have borne,
You are the deliverance of the faithful who seek your help.
Open to us the gates of your compassion, Blessed Mother of God.
As we have placed our hope in you, may we never be put to confusion;
But through you may we be delivered from all adversity.

THE SEAL

+ Through the prayers of our holy Fathers and Mothers,
    Lord Jesus Christ our God, have mercy on us and save us. Amen.

*If a feeling of despondency "catches" the heart and endures over a time, gently
and calmly repeat the recurring phrase: "Lord Jesus have mercy on me," or
"Lord give me your light."*

*Simple and direct phrases like this, calmly and hopefully repeated, beneath
the breath, as we go on about other things in our daily life (like the blind man
on the Jericho Road, or like the Syrophoenician woman following after Jesus)
can serve to replace other long prayers for which, when one feels despondent,
one may not have the heart.*

*As Scripture says (Ps. 33:19) (Ps. 34 in English Bibles): "God is close to
the broken-hearted. And those whose spirit is crushed he himself will save."
An appropriate Psalm of Thanksgiving when the spirit of despondency lifts is
contained in Psalm 29 LXX ("I will praise you, Lord, you have rescued me").*

Thanksgiving Prayers in Time of Joy

THE OPENING BLESSING

+ Blessed is our God, + always now and ever and to the ages of ages. Amen.

Glory to you, our God, glory to you.

(or the "Seal")

THE TRISAGION PRAYERS
(repeat from pages 8–9)

INVITATORY PRAYER

+ Come let us worship and bow down before God our King.
  (bowing low each time)
+ Come let us worship and bow down before Christ, our King and God.
+ Come let us worship and bow down before Christ himself, our King and our God.

Psalm 32

Ring out your joy to the Lord, O you just;
For praise is fitting for loyal hearts.

Give thanks to the Lord upon the harp,
With a ten-stringed lute sing him songs.

O sing him a song that is new,
Play loudly, with all your skill.

For the word of the Lord is faithful
And all his works to be trusted.

The Lord loves justice and right
And fills the earth with his love.

By his word the heavens were made,
By the breath of his mouth all the stars.

He collects the waves of the ocean;
He stores up the depths of the sea.

Let all the earth fear the Lord
All who live in the world revere him.

He spoke; and it came to be.
He commanded; it sprang into being.

He frustrates the designs of the nations,
He defeats the plans of the peoples.

His own designs shall stand for ever,
The plans of his heart from age to age.

They are happy, whose God is the Lord,
The people he has chosen as his own.

From the heavens the Lord looks forth,
He sees all the children of earth.

From the place where he dwells he gazes
On all the dwellers on the earth;

He who shapes the hearts of them all;
And considers all their deeds.

A king is not saved by his army,
Nor are warriors preserved by their strength.

A vain hope for safety is the horse;
Despite its power it cannot save.

The Lord looks on those who revere him,
On those who hope in his love,

To rescue their souls from death,
To keep them alive in famine.

Our soul is waiting for the Lord.
The Lord is our help and our shield.

In him do our hearts find joy.
We trust in his holy name.

May your love be upon us, O Lord,
As we place all our hope in you.

Psalm 46

All peoples, clap your hands,
Cry to God with shouts of joy!

For the Lord, the Most High, we must fear,
Great king over all the earth.

He subdues peoples under us
And nations under our feet.

Our inheritance, our glory, is from him,
Given to Jacob out of love.

God goes up with shouts of joy;
The Lord goes up with trumpet blast.

Sing praise for God, sing praise,
Sing praise to our king, sing praise.

God is king of all the earth,
Sing praise with all your skill.

God is king over the nations;
God reigns on his holy throne.

The princes of the people are assembled
With the people of Abraham's God.

The rulers of the earth belong to God,
To God who reigns over all.

Psalm 99

Cry out with joy to the Lord, all the earth.
Serve the Lord with gladness.

Come before him, singing for joy.
Know that he, the Lord, is God.

He made us, we belong to him,
We are his people, the sheep of his flock.

Go within his gates, giving thanks.
Enter his courts with songs of praise.

Give thanks to him and bless his name.
Indeed, how good is the Lord,

Eternal his merciful love.
He is faithful from age to age.

This would be a very appropriate place, if desired, to insert the Prayer of St. Nicetas—the Te Deum—from the section "Prayers of the Ancient Saints."

+ Glory to the Father, and to the Son, and to the Holy Spirit. Now and ever and to the ages of ages. Amen.

+ Alleluia, Alleluia, Alleluia, glory to you, O Lord. *(three times)*

PRAYER OF THANKSGIVING

We give thanks to you, Lord, merciful God and Father of Lights. For you have always watched over us, always intent on leading us into the good and establishing us in the radiant light of your face. We thank you for all the innumerable benefits that we have received from your goodness: things seen and unseen, those things we know and the multitudes of things we do not know. And we, your grateful servants, give you glory, thanksgiving, and honor: + to the Father, and to the Son, and to the Holy Spirit. Now and ever and to the ages of ages. Amen.

READING FROM THE HOLY GOSPEL

Jesus lifted up his eyes to heaven and said, "Father, the hour has come; glorify your Son that the Son may glorify you, for you have given him dominion over all flesh, so as to gift eternal life to all whom you have given him. And this is eternal life, that they should know you, the only true God, and Jesus Christ whom you have sent. I glorified you on earth, accomplishing the work that you gave me to do; and now, Father, glorify me in your own presence with the glory I had with you before the world was made. I revealed your name to those you gave me from out of the world. They were yours, and you gave them to me, and they have kept your word. Now they know that everything that you have given me comes indeed from you, for I have given them the words you gave to me, and they have received them and truly know that I came from you. They have believed that it was you who sent me. I am praying for them; I am not praying for the world but for those whom you have given me, for they belong to you. All that is mine belongs to you. All that is yours belongs to me; and I am glorified in them. As from now I am no more in this world, but they are in the world. I am coming to you. Holy Father, keep them in your name, which you have given me, that they may be one, even as we are one. While I was with them, I kept them in your name, which you have given me. I guarded them, and not one of them was lost except the son of perdition, which was the fulfillment of the Scripture. But now I am coming to you; and I say these things while in the world, so that they may have my own joy completed in themselves." (Jn. 17:1–13)

LITANY OF INTERCESSION

In peace let us pray to the Lord.	Lord have mercy
For the church of God across the face of the earth	Lord have mercy
For all who live faithfully, seeking Christ's will	Lord have mercy
For the suffering and the homeless	Lord have mercy
For captives and their salvation	Lord have mercy
For the oppressed and their deliverance	Lord have mercy
For the sick and the despairing	Lord have mercy
For those who have suffered loss or great sorrow	Lord have mercy
For our strengthening in joy and hope	Lord have mercy
For . . . *(the names and causes we wish to pray for)*	Lord have mercy
For all of us who call on you from our hearts	Lord have mercy
	Lord have mercy
	Lord have mercy

PRAYER TO THE MOTHER OF GOD

You are more honorable than the Cherubim and incomparably more glorious than the Seraphim, for as a virgin you gave birth to God the Word. Truly Mother of God, we magnify you.

In awe at the beauty of your virginity, Mother of God,
And the immense radiance of your purity,
Gabriel cried out before you:
What fitting hymn of praise can I offer you?
How should I address you?
I stand in awe and hesitate,
And thus, as I was commanded, I cry out to you:
Rejoice, who are so full of grace!

THE SEAL

+ Through the prayers of our holy Fathers and Mothers,
   Lord Jesus Christ our God, have mercy on us and save us. Amen.

Various Prayers for Specific Occasions

INVOCATION FOR THE DESCENT
OF THE HOLY SPIRIT

(raising one's hands to heaven)

O Lord, who at the third hour sent down your Holy Spirit on the apostles,
Do not take him from us, O Good One, but renew him in us who pray
to you:

(bowing down low to the ground)

+ Create in me a clean heart, O God, and put a new and constant spirit
within me.

(raising one's hands to heaven)

O Lord, who at the third hour sent down your Holy Spirit on the apostles,
Do not take him from us, O Good One, but renew him in us who pray
to you:

(bowing down low to the ground)

+ Cast me not from your presence and do not deprive me of your Holy
Spirit.

(raising one's hands to heaven)

O Lord, who at the third hour sent down your Holy Spirit on the apostles,
Do not take him from us, O Good One, but renew him in us who pray
to you:

(bowing down low to the ground)

+ Glory to the Father, and to the Son, and to the Holy Spirit. Now and ever and to the ages of ages. Amen.

Liturgy of St. John Chrysostom (345–407)

FOR THE GRACE OF THE HOLY SPIRIT

O Heavenly King, the Paraclete, Spirit of Truth who are present everywhere, filling all things, Treasury of Good and Giver of Life, come and dwell in us, cleanse us of every stain, and save our souls, O Good One.

Orthodox Book of Hours

FOR THE NEW DAY

Lord our God, we give you thanks, for you have wakened us from a restful sleep by your gracious mercy. Now waken our minds to righteousness for your sake, O Lord, that our eyes may see your salvation. We are your servants; may your divinity come to dwell in us; may your mercy shelter and protect us. May we who serve you meditate day and night on the love of your commandments, give you constant thanks, and glorify you: Father, Son, and Holy Spirit, now and ever and to the ages of ages. Amen.

St. John Mantakuni (Catholicos of Armenia 420–490)

INVOCATION OF THE MOTHER OF GOD AT TIME OF PRAYER

The memory of Mary is our blessing;

May her prayer be a confirmation of our souls.

Blessed are you, our proud delight.

Blessed are you, our house of refuge.

Blessed are you who became the Mother of God.

The air is full of the fragrance of your presence,

Virgin Mary, Mother of God,

For you bore your maker, the Lord of all the earth.

Neither among virgins nor prophets,

Not in pure gold or in any form of beauty

Is there a loveliness to compare with yours, Mother of God.

Intercede for us now who call upon you.

Syriac Slawoto: Book of Prayers

INVOCATION OF A SAINT AT TIME OF PRAYER

Your memory is more radiant than the sun, and more lovely than the moon, blessed holy *(father or mother)* –X–, for the sun gives its light by day, and the moon by night, but your beauty shines over the church ceaselessly. Come and pray with us. You are like a tree that grows by running water, whose crown reaches to the heavens, whose fruits give sustenance to all. Come now and pray with us.

Syriac Slawoto: Book of Prayers

BEFORE TRAVELING

Lord Jesus Christ, you are the pathway to all truth and the guide of our life. It was you who led Joseph safely to Egypt and the Israelites through the Red Sea. You led Moses to Mount Sinai and all his people to the Promised Land. It was you yourself who traveled at the side of Cleopas and his companion to Emmaus. Today I pray you, Lord, lead me and my loved ones safely on this journey that lies before us. Save us from all enemies, visible or invisible, and bring us safely to our destination: for you are our way, our truth, and our life, and to you we give glory and worship, now and ever and to the ages of ages. Amen.

St. John Garnetsi, the Armenian (1180–1245)

BEFORE COMMUNION

At your Mystical Supper, O Son of God, receive me this day as a communicant; for I will not speak of your Mystery to your enemies, nor like Judas will I give you a kiss, but like the thief I will confess you: "Remember me, O Lord, in your kingdom."

Liturgy of St. John Chrysostom (345–407)

AFTER COMMUNION

O Lord Jesus Christ, my God, let your holy body be my eternal life, and your precious blood, the remission of my sins. May this Eucharist be my joy, my health, and my gladness. Make me, a sinner, worthy to stand at the right hand of your glory at your awesome Second Coming, through the prayers of your Most Pure Mother and of all the saints. Amen.

Liturgy of St. John Chrysostom (345–407)

FOR A LOVED ONE WHO HAS DIED

O God of spirits and of all flesh, you who have trampled down death, overthrown the evil one, and given life to your world: Lord, now give rest to the soul of your departed servant –X– in a place of refreshment, a place of repose, a place from which all sorrow and sighing have been banished. Pardon them every transgression that they may have committed, in word, or deed, or thought; for you are a Good God who loves mankind, and indeed there is no one who lives and does not sin, for you alone are without sin, and your righteousness is everlasting, and your word is truth.

Orthodox Funeral Service

HYMN OF REPENTANCE

Christ my true God have mercy on me.
In iniquity was I conceived,
And so, my Savior, have mercy on me.
Do not cast me aside. But have mercy on me.
By his heartfelt sighing the tax collector was heard
And received forgiveness in the temple.
Using his words I too cry out:
Lord, my God, have mercy on me.
The thief cried out upon his cross: "Remember me Lord."
Using his words I too cry out:
Lord, my God, have mercy on me.
The prodigal son beseeched you with the words:
"Father I have sinned before heaven and before you."
Using his words I too cry out:
Lord, my God, have mercy on me.

St. Mesrob Mashtots of Armenia (ca. 404)

EVENING PRAYER OF REPENTANCE

Lord, I stand knocking at the door of your compassion,
Seeking your forgiveness.
By evil I have been kept from the path of life.
My mouth has not praised you;
My feet have not walked in your holy place.
Lover of our race, have pity on me.
You who are the splendor of the Father give light to my eyes
That I may give thanks for your grace.
I have lain in darkness in this deceit-filled world.
Morning has passed and I did not repent.
Evening has fallen and my sins have increased.
But let your compassion now ascend before my face.

Syriac Slawoto: Book of Prayers

GRACE BEFORE MEALS

+ In the name of the Father, and of the Son, and of the Holy Spirit.
  Bless us, O Lord, and these your gifts we are about to receive
  through your goodness, through Christ our Lord Amen.

Roman Ritual

+ In the name of the Father, and of the Son, and of the Holy Spirit.
  Christ our God, + bless the food and drink of us your servants,
  For you are holy, always, now, and ever, and to the ages of
  ages. Amen.

Orthodox Book of Hours

GRACE AFTER MEALS

+ In the name of the Father, and of the Son, and of the Holy Spirit.

   We give you thanks, O Christ our God,

   For you have filled us with these good things of the earth.

   Do not deprive us of your heavenly kingdom,

   But as you were present among your disciples, O Savior,

   And gave them peace,

   So also come among us and save our souls.

Orthodox Book of Hours

FOR GUIDANCE WHEN MAKING IMPORTANT CHANGES IN LIFE

Lord and Master, you know well that I scarcely know what is good for me, but now that I am thinking about beginning on this new venture, how will I know it is right unless you yourself guide me with your grace? Grant me, Lord, your guidance in all things related to this matter, so that I do not simply follow my personal inclinations and come to grief; but rather you yourself guide me and hold me safe so that what I do will be in accordance with your good will. If this plan is good in your eyes, give me your blessing to bring it to a successful end. If it is not, then remove the desire for it from my heart. You know all things, Lord, and nothing is concealed from you. I am your servant; deal with me as you see right, for I know that I can never win peace or success unless I join myself to your blessed will. Teach me, Lord, to say on each occasion: "Not as I will, but as you will." + For yours is the kingdom and the power and the glory; of the Father, and of the Son, and of the Holy Spirit. Now and ever and to the ages of ages. Amen.

Coptic Book of Hours

INTERCESSION FOR THE GRACE OF PRAYER

Lord our God, you gave your peace to us and sent down upon your disciples and apostles the gift of the Holy Spirit, whose power opened their lips by tongues of fire. Now open the lips of us who are sinners, and teach us how to pray, and what to pray for. Direct us in all things, for you are the calm harbor of all who are driven by the tempests of this life. Make us know how we ought to live. Renew your good Spirit within us, and in him let our sliding thoughts find stability, so that day by day we may be guided into what is right and be found worthy to fulfill your commandments, and always have the memory of your glorious and longed-for presence among us. Lord, do not allow us to be deceived by the facile allurements of our time, but strengthen us so that we can reach out to grasp the treasures of the age to come: + for you are blessed and praised, in the company of your saints, to the ages of ages. Amen.

St. Basil the Great (330–379)

THE SONG OF THE BEATITUDES

In your kingdom, remember us, O Lord,

When you come into your kingdom.

Blessed are the poor in spirit, for theirs is the kingdom of heaven.

Blessed are those who mourn, for they shall be comforted.

Blessed are the meek, for they shall inherit the earth.

Blessed are those who hunger and thirst after righteousness, for they shall be filled.

Blessed are the merciful, for they shall obtain mercy.

Blessed are the pure in heart, for they shall see God.

Blessed are the peacemakers, for they shall be called children of God.

Blessed are those who are persecuted for righteousness' sake, for theirs is the kingdom of heaven.

Blessed are you when men shall revile you and persecute you,

And shall say all manner of evil against you falsely for my sake.

Rejoice and be exceedingly glad, for great is your reward in heaven!

Liturgy of St. John Chrysostom (345–407)

FOR THE NEW DAY

Lord, grant me the strength to greet the coming day in peace.

Help me in everything to rely on your holy will.

Show your will to me every hour of the day.

Bless my dealings with all people.

Teach me to treat those who come to me throughout the day with peace of soul, and with the firm conviction that it is your will that governs all things.

Guide my thoughts and feelings in everything I do and everything I say.

In unexpected events let me not forget that all have been sent by you.

Teach me to act wisely and firmly, without embittering or embarrassing others.

Give me the physical strength to bear the labors of this day.

Direct my will. Teach me to pray: rather, yourself pray within me.

St. Philaret, Metropolitan of Moscow (19th cent.)

AT A GRAVESIDE

Master, Lord our God, it is through your mercy that the souls of the faithful departed are given their rest. Bless this grave of your servant —X— and set a holy angel to guard over it, that the body which is buried here may find it a place of gentle repose even until your Second Coming in glory, and the hour of the resurrection. Grant that our souls may be delivered from all their bonds of sin and discover eternal joy in the company of the saints in your heavenly court. For you are the King of this world and the Savior of our souls and bodies, and to you we ascribe glory: + to the Father, and to the Son, and to the Holy Spirit. Now and ever and to the ages of ages. Amen.

Orthodox Book of Rituals

ON RECEIVING A NEW VEHICLE

(Psalm 90 may be recited also.)

Lord our God, who sit upon the Cherubim and ride upon the Seraphim, you have given us wisdom out of your own goodness of heart, that it may always guide us in safe and proper ways. Send down your blessing upon this vehicle + and appoint an angel to watch over it, so that all who travel within it may be protected and guided in peace. May they always act in accordance with your gift of wisdom; so that setting out with your blessing, they may return from their journeys giving thanks for your providence and praising you: Father, Son, and Holy Spirit, now and ever and to the ages of ages. Amen.

Orthodox Book of Rituals

PART 3

Prayers of the Ancient Saints

The saints of the ancient church are to this day, among Christians, venerated not only as teachers but also as living vessels of the Spirit. They were proven in fidelity to God and consecrated as vessels of his Spirit and have been given a special place in the light of the kingdom. In the church's experience, they are not "dead and gone," but living heralds of Christ's truth and grace, and active for the good in the communion of the saints, which includes us here on earth. In its daily prayers, the church often calls to them. The Syriac Orthodox have the following graceful prayer in their ritual books, to invoke the assistance of a saint in time of prayer: "Your memory is more radiant than the sun, and more lovely than the moon, Blessed One, for the sun gives its light by day, and the moon by night, but your beauty shines over the church ceaselessly. Come and pray with us. You are like a tree that grows by running water, whose crown reaches to the heavens, whose fruits give sustenance to all. Come now and pray with us."[7]

The prayers from the ancient saints gathered here are offered as classic examples of prayer. Those who were powerful in the ways of the Spirit while they lived can give us masterful demonstrations of how to call on the Spirit in our own time. Many of the following prayers are truly ancient in character and open up for us an intimate portrait of how the early church lifted up its heart and soul in prayer. Many of the ones chosen here are quite evidently high works of poetry and hymnology. Some of them were composed by the greatest of the Christian poets: writers such as Gregory the Theologian (Nazianzen) or Symeon the New Theologian, or the Latin master Prudentius. These highly crafted and most elegant prayer poems exemplify the spirit of the ancient church: that prayer is beautiful in and of itself, because it is imbued with the presence of the One it seeks, who is Supreme Beauty.

PRAYER OF ST. IOANNIKIOS *(9th cent.)*

My hope is the Father.
My refuge is the Son.
My shelter is the Holy Spirit.
O Holy Trinity, glory to you.

EUCHARISTIC PRAYER OF ST. JUSTIN
MARTYR *(2nd cent.)*

We give thanks to you, our Father,
For the holy vine of your servant David,
Which you made known to us through Jesus your Servant.
We thank you, Father,
For the life and understanding that you made known to us
Through Jesus your Servant.
To you be glory for ever.
Just as the broken bread was once scattered over the hills
And was gathered together to be made one,
So let your church be gathered together
Out of the ends of the earth,
And into your kingdom.
For yours is the glory and the power,
Through Jesus the Christ, forever.

PRAYER FOR COMPASSION
(From a 2nd-cent. papyrus of Berlin)

Benefactor of all who look to you,
Light of those who dwell in darkness,

Creator of each seed,

Gardener of every spiritual plant,

Take pity upon me, my Lord,

And make me into a pure temple.

Do not judge me according to my sins,

For if you should mark my offenses

I could no longer stand before you.

But because of your immense compassion and infinite mercy,

Cleanse me in the name of our Lord Jesus Christ,

Your Only Son, who is the most sacred Healer of our souls.

And to you, through him, be every glory, power, honor, and magnificence

In the endless ages of ageless ages. Amen.

HYMN OF GLORY   *(Codex Alexandrinus, 4th cent.)*

Glory to God on high, and

Peace on earth to all of good will.

We praise you,

We bless you,

We adore you,

We glorify you,

We give you thanks for your great glory

O Lord,

Celestial King,

All-Powerful God,

The Savior,

The Only Son,

Jesus Christ,

And the Holy Spirit.

Lord God,

Lamb of God, Son of the Father,

Who washes away the sins of the world,

Have mercy on us.

Hear our prayer,

You who sit at the right hand of the Father,

And have mercy on us.

For you alone are holy,

You alone are Lord,

Jesus Christ,

To the glory of God the Father. Amen.

PRAYER OF ST. BASIL THE GREAT *(4th cent.)*

God and Master, Lord Jesus Christ, the source of life and immortality, who made all creation, seen and unseen, the Son who along with the Father are eternal and without beginning, in these last days out of the abundance of your love, you put on flesh, were crucified and killed for our sake, ungrateful and careless even as we are. By your own blood you remade our nature that had been corrupted by sin. Immortal King, now accept my sinner's repentance, bend down your ear to me to hear my prayer, for I have sinned, Lord. I have sinned against heaven and before you, and I am not worthy to look upon the height of your glory.

I have provoked your goodness by breaking your commandments and not obeying your decrees, but you, O Lord, are patient, and long-suffering, and full of mercy, and have not abandoned me to the destructiveness of my evil, but have constantly waited for my conversion. It was you, the Lover of Humankind, who said through your prophet: "I do not desire the death of a sinner, rather that they should be converted and love." For you did not wish the work of your own hands to perish, Master, nor did you find any delight in the destruction of mortal kind, rather desiring all to be saved and to come to the knowledge of the truth.

And so, even though I am unworthy of both heaven and earth, since I have become the slave of sin and addicted myself to pleasure, defacing your image within, nevertheless, I am your work and your creation and even though I am wretched I do not despair of my salvation, for I am made bold because of your immeasurable compassion, and so I draw near. Therefore, my Christ, Lover of Humanity, receive even me, as you once received the sinful woman, the tax collector, and the prodigal son. Lift away the heavy burden of my sins, you who take away the sins of the world and heal all our infirmities. For you did not come to call the righteous, but to call sinners to repentance; and you call to your side those who labor and are heavy-burdened, so as to give them rest. And so, cleanse me of all defilement of flesh and spirit, and teach me to arrive at holiness in reverencing you.

PRAYER OF ST. SERAPION OF THMUIS *(4th cent.)*

We thank you, God our Master,
That you have called us back together though we wandered,
And brought us sinners back to yourself,
Setting aside the judgment that stood against us,
Wiping it away because of our repentance,
Casting it aside because we came to know you,
Who had pity upon us out of your great philanthropy.

PRAYER OF ST. NICETAS *(Te Deum, 5th cent.)*

We praise you as God;
We confess you to be Lord.
All the earth worships you, Father Everlasting.
All the angels [and archangels] cry out to you,
The heavens and all the powers they contain.
To you the Cherubim and Seraphim ceaselessly sing:
Holy, Holy, Holy, Lord God of Hosts,
Heaven and earth are full of the majesty of your glory.
The glorious company of the apostles praises you.
The godly ranks of the prophets offer you praise.
The white-clad army of martyrs praises you.
Your holy church across the world turns to you:
Father of infinite majesty,
The Honorable, True, and Only Begotten Son,
The Holy Spirit, the Paraclete.

SALVE REGINA *(Roman Ritual, 12th cent.)*

Hail Queen and Mother of Mercy,
Our life, our sweetness, and our hope.
To you we cry, the exiled children of Eve,
To you we turn with sighs,
Lamenting and weeping,
In this Vale of Tears.
Be our Advocate;
Turn to us those gracious eyes of yours
And after this, our time of exile, ends
Show to us that blessed fruit of your womb, Jesus.
For you are merciful and holy, sweet Virgin Mary.

PRAYER OF ST. EPHREM *(4th cent.)*

Lord and Master of my Life:
Take from me the spirit of sloth,
Despondency, lust for power, and idle talk. *(bowing low)*
And give your servant instead
A spirit of chastity, humility, forbearing, and love. *(bowing low)*
O Lord my King,
Grant that I might see my own shortcomings
And not judge my fellows:
For blessed are you to the ages of ages. *(bowing low)* Amen.

HYMN TO THE SPIRIT OF GOD

(Veni Creator Spiritus, Rabanus Maurus, 9th cent.)

Come Creator Spirit
To our deepest mind, your home
You who made our inmost hearts,
Fill them with your heavenly grace.
Your title is the Paraclete,
Gift of God Most High;
Living Spring, and Fire, and Love,
Spiritual anointment.
You, who are sevenfold in your gifts,
Finger of God's right hand,
According to the Father's promise
You gift our lips with speech.
Come set brightness in our senses,
Pour love into our hearts,

Strengthen our failing bodies
With your unfailing power.
Drive far away the Enemy,
And soon bring us back to peace.
With you before us on the path
We shall avoid all danger.
Grant us knowledge of the Father
And knowledge of the Son, through you,
Who are ever Spirit of them both,
As our faith declares.
All glory to the Father
And to the Risen Son
And to the Paraclete,
From age to age. Amen.

MORNING HYMN

(Aterne Rerum Conditor, St. Ambrose, 4th cent.)

Eternal maker of all things,
Who rule both day and night,
And set the bounds on time itself,
As respite for our frailty,
The herald of the day now sounds,
Watchful in the depth of night,
Telling travelers that first light has come,
Cutting off each night from night.
Thereby the Bringer of Light is roused
And frees the skies of darkness.
At his cry a throng of ills
Leave off their evil ways.

At this the sailor gains new strength

And raging seas subside.

Hearing his song, the church's rock

Washed off his guilt in tears.

So let us rise with gladness.

The cockerel rouses those abed,

And scolds all tired laggards,

Shouting down who would resist.

At the cockerel's call, our hope renews,

The sick find health restored,

The robber's sword is sheathed,

The lapsed find faith again.

Jesus, look on our frail state

And by your gaze correct us.

If you look on, our faults shall fall,

And guilt dissolve in tears.

Lord of light, shine on our sense;

Scatter phantoms of our mind.

Our voice shall hymn you first this day,

Offering you our prayers and vows.

EVENING HYMN *(Greek Liturgy, 3rd cent.)*

Jesus Christ

The Gladdening Light

Of the deathless Father's holy glory;

The heavenly, holy, blessed One.

As the sun reclines, we see the light of evening,

And sing our hymn to God:

The Father, Son, and Holy Spirit.

Worthy are you, O Son of God,
Through each and every moment,
That joyful songs should hymn you.
You are the Giver of our life,
And so the world gives glory.

CAEDMON'S HYMN *(7th cent.)*

Now it is time to sing praise
To high heaven's Guardian,
Tell the deeds of the Father of Glory,
That Everlasting Lord,
Beginning of every wonder.
First that holy Maker
Crafted heaven as a roof
For the children of Adam.
Next, the Keeper of Mankind
Furnished earth below,
A good land for us.
That Almighty God and Everlasting Lord.

CHERUBIC HYMN *(Greek Liturgy, 6th cent.)*

We stand as mystic symbols of the Cherubim
And offer the thrice-holy hymn
To the Trinity that gives all life.
Now set aside all earth-bound care
And receive the King of All
Escorted round

By unseen ranks of angels.
Alleluia. Alleluia. Alleluia.

EUCHARISTIC HYMN *(Greek Liturgy, 9th cent.)*

This day receive me, Son of God,
Communing at your mystic feast.
For I will not betray
Your Mystery to your foes:
Will never give a kiss
Like that which Judas gave.
But like the thief
I shall confess to you:
In your royal kingdom, Lord,
Be mindful then of me.

EVENING HYMN *(Pseudo-Ambrose, 5th cent.)*

Blessed Light of Trinity,
Originating Unity,
Now as the fiery sun declines
Pour radiance in our hearts.
In morning songs we offered praise;
At evening we implore you.
To you, our glory,
Through every age,
We, your suppliants, offer praise.

IN PRAISE OF THE PASSION OF CHRIST

(Flavius Merobaudes, 5th cent.)

True Child of God, more ancient than all years,
You entered in our race, to show the face of God;
And break the grip of that subtle error
Held through many an age,
Seducing human hearts.
How gracefully you freed our souls from sin.
On spent bodies, restoring vital breath where it had failed.
You passed, Immortal, to the Land of Shades,
Breaking in the secret place of death.
You alone, Immortal One,
Flinging back the veil of night
Rose on high to the Father in heaven
And by your everlasting plan
Purged evil from the face of earth.
You alone stand with the Father,
And you, that Spirit wholly pure,
Who all are One Simplicity
In threefold light.
And thus we stand in wonder
That for our sakes alone
The holder of the power of life
Came even to his death.

(VEGETARIAN) HYMN OF
GRACE BEFORE MEALS

(Prudentius, 5th cent.)

Kind Lord who bore the cross,

Source of all our light.

All-creative, Gracious, Word-begot,

Now made flesh within the Virgin's womb,

Yet mighty in your Father, first,

Before the stars, or earth, or seas, were made:

Turn your saving face, I pray,

Upon this copious scene,

That with your peace, and in your light,

And under your ennobling name,

We may enjoy this food.

Without you, Lord, is nothing sweet.

All that we taste is dust:

Unless our food and drink

Are flavored first by sanctifying faith,

Tinged with Christ's sweet favor.

So, let our simple bread bear God's own salt;

May Christ flow within our cups,

May the threefold holiness above

Direct our sober words and jests,

Our laughter and our talk,

All that we do and all we are.

Such opulence for Christians is enough

And satisfies all needs.

Far from us that hungering lust

That craves a bloody feast,

And tears apart the flesh of beasts.

Such wild banquets, made from slaughtered flocks,
Are fit only for barbarians.
For us, the olive, wheat, and ripening fruits,
And vegetables of every kind:
These compose our righteous feast.

HYMN AT THE EVENING LIGHTING OF THE LAMPS *(Prudentius, 5th cent.)*

Gracious Lord, Creator of the golden light,
You establish the patterns of revolving time,
And as the sun now sets,
The gloom of night advances in.
For all your faithful, Christ, restore the light!
You have arrayed the heavenly court
With all its countless stars,
Setting the moon there as a lamp,
Yet still have shown us how to seek
Those lights whose seeds spring out
Whenever stony flint is struck.
This was to teach mankind a hope
Which light bestowed on us
When Christ came with his own flesh.
For, as he said, he is that steadfast rock,
From which a fire sprang forth to all our race.
This tiny flame we nurse in lamps
Brimming with rich and fragrant oil,
Or on the dry timber of a torch,
Or on the rushlights we have made,
Steeped in wax pressed from the comb.

The flickering light grows strong
As the hollow earthenware lamp
Yields up its richness to the thirsty wick,
As the pine branch drips its nourishing sap,
And the fire drinks the warmth of waxen tapers down.
Drop by drop, in perfumed tears,
The glowing, liquid nectar falls.
The eager fire sends forth rain
As burning waxen candles
Weep themselves away.
It is by your own gifts, Father,
Our halls are gleaming now with dancing lights
That strive to emulate departed day,
While conquered Night withdraws in flight,
Rending her dark cloak as she runs.
Lord, you are the true light of our eyes,
And light to all our senses,
That which we see within, and that which lies without.
Accept this light I offer up to you
As my evening worship, Lord,
A light that brims with perfumed oils of peace.
Most Holy Father, through Christ your Son,
Your glory stands revealed:
Your Only-Born, Our Lord,
Who breathed the Spirit over us,
Out of the bosom of the Father.
Through him your glory, honor, praise, and wisdom,
Your goodness, gracefulness, and might,
Endure in your kingdom, thrice-holy God,
And spread through ages of the everlasting ages. Amen.

GRACE BEFORE EATING

(Anonymous Byzantine, 5th cent.)

Blessed are You, O Lord,
Who have fed me from my youth,
And give all flesh their food.
Fill us with joy and gladness,
That having all we need,
we might abound in good works
In Jesus Christ our Lord:
With whom, to you be glory,
Honor, and dominion,
To the ages of the ages. Amen.

EVENING PRAYER

(Anonymous Byzantine, 5th cent.)

Receive the prayers,
Thrice-holy Savior,
Of those who stand on earth to hymn you.
Look down with sleepless eye,
O Lover of the human race,
And overlook our weakness,
And grant us peaceful rest.
Receive our prayer,
Raise up our souls,
Lest our faults impede our prayer.
Deliver us, your servants,
From the grief of Judgment,
And make us worthy,

Who sing to you now,
To stand in the choir of the saints.

+ Glory to the Father, and to the Son, and to the Holy Spirit.
Now and ever and to the ages of ages. Amen.

EVENING HYMN OF THE RESURRECTION

(St. John Damascene, 8th cent.)

Most Holy Lord,
Receive our evening prayers
And grant us forgiveness of our sins.
None else but you has shown within this world
The Holy Resurrection.
"Go round Zion, you nations,
And encircle her."
Give glory within her
To him who rose from the dead,
Who is himself our very God,
Who out of the midst of all our sins
Has redeemed each and every one.
Come, my people, let us sing a hymn
Venerating Christ,
To glorify his resurrection from the dead.
He is our very God
And has redeemed the World
From all the Enemy's deceit.

HYMN IN HONOR OF THE VIRGIN MARY

(St. John Damascene, 8th cent.)

Let us sing a hymn
To Mary the Virgin
That Heavenly Gate
And Glory of our World,
The New Bud of Humankind
Who gave birth to the Lord.
Of her the angels make their song,
The proud boast of all the church,
For she received within herself
No less than heaven,
And is the Temple of our God.
For she "has broken down
The dividing wall of enmity":
Has brought about our peace;
Opened access to the throne of God.
Hold fast to her, the Anchor of our Faith.
We have as a Mighty Champion
Her who from her very self
Gave to the Lord his birth.
And so, take heart,
Take heart you people of God,
For he himself shall gird for war
Against our many foes,
Who is the Lover of the Human Race.

HYMN TO THE LIFE-GIVING CROSS

(St. John Damascene, 8th cent.)

O Christ our God,
Ceaselessly we bow
Before your cross
That gives us life;
And glorify your Resurrection,
Most powerful Lord,
When on that third day
You made anew
The failing nature of mankind,
Showing us revealed
The path to heaven above:
For you alone are good,
The Lover of the Human Race.

HYMN TO THE DIVINE LOVE

(St. Symeon the New Theologian, 11th cent.)

Your beauty is astounding.
Your face is beyond compare.
Your splendor is ineffable.
Your glory, all word transcends.
Your sweet kindness, O Christ our Master,
Exceeds our faltering earthy thoughts,
And this is why our longing,
And the love we feel for you
Outshines all love and desire
We mortals can ever know on earth.

The Jesus Prayer
PRAYER OF THE HEART

The Prayer of the Heart is an ancient practice of the church. The Jesus Prayer is one of the most common ways to enter into that prayer: when the mind has retreated into the quietness of the heart, and the heart itself has entered deep within the body to "know" (for the "heart" means spiritual awareness in the Scriptures more than it means emotion) that we are in the temple of the soul: the holy place where God meets each one of us in the inmost sanctuary of the self. The Jesus Prayer can be stated in a few lines: *Lord Jesus Christ, Son of God, have mercy on me*. If one says it in a group, one person can lead it, ending with: "Have mercy on us" instead. Many prayer groups engage in the Jesus Prayer, using this short phrase for a half hour or forty-five minutes at a time. It is the focal point of several monastic evening services of prayer. It can be easily stated, but it takes a lifetime to sound its depths. It is the door of words to the silent prayer of the heart, which is by nature wordless. At first, the Jesus Prayer needs to be recited slowly, most calmly, in a most heart-centered way. In the end, the words on the lips will be simply a toy for the restless body and the mind's imaginative faculties, while the heart and soul take a rest in order to commune with the Lord. The Holy Name evokes this mystic quietness. That rest or quietness (it is called *hesychia* in Greek) has a deep theological tradition behind it known as Byzantine Hesychasm. It is not to be confused with the early-modern phenomenon known as "Quietism."[8]

I think not much more can be spoken about the prayer of the heart generically. To embark upon it is to leave all books behind, except the script the Spirit writes on the pages of the heart. This, of course, is the real heart and soul of prayer. But it is something so elevated, intimate, and personal that it cannot be the "bread and butter" of our common and regular prayers (at least not for most of us making our pilgrimage in this modern world). And that is why a book of prayers such as this one, along with regular habits of prayer, is so important. Nevertheless, we should always remember that the heart and soul of prayer lie there in the heights, which are also the inmost depths. And so, the Jesus Prayer is a powerful supplement, a good beginning—or better, end—to any of the services contained in this book. If one wishes to engage in it, then stand quietly, or kneel down comfortably. Give voice to the words of the prayer very slowly, very softly. Do not give the mind much to do, or the body for that matter, apart from the recitation. If the mind wants to think its many thoughts at the front of your head (and it will!), turn it for the first few minutes to the words themselves, and keep doing this whenever imaginations assert themselves once more; but do so with the intention of "settling the mind with the words," not meditating on the meaning of the prayer words as such. They can stand years of exegesis: for they are a synopsis of the Lord's own parable of the tax collector and the publican, and they call to mind also the blind man outside Jericho crying out for salvation as the Lord made his way to his Passion. They are the synopsis of all our Christian faith: for no one is able to call on Jesus as Lord except in the Holy Spirit, as the Apostle taught us. But in prayer it is not the time for such exegesis.

Allow the words to form a wave, building up and crashing down. The prayer when vocalized (as it should be for the first while) makes it very hard to do this "physically" (one cannot breathe in and out while speaking) so just regard it as a guide that will make more sense when the prayer eventually becomes (as it will soon enough) not so much vocalized as sotto voce. The wave comes in two parts: the first is the "Lord Jesus Christ, Son of God," breathed in as the invocation of the Holy Name into the deep self. The second is the "Have mercy on me (us)," breathed out as a suspiration. The wave of the phrases reflects the breathing of the one who prays. It is not so important to make this correspond exactly, as monastics do who have had many years' practice and who also benefit from deeply experienced guides close at hand. It is more important to allow the breathing to become symbolically synchronized with the recitation: and so the reciting of the words should be slow and calm as is the breathing: never rushed and agitated. The prayer must be slow and calm, therefore; the breathing should reflect us in a calm and peaceful state. Practice getting the words slower and slower until they are right, moving the prism of the lips until the rainbow beam appears at just that right diffraction. The constant call for mercy is not meant to be evocative of a guilt-neurosis; rather, it is designed to evoke a heartfelt desire to know God in the light of his mercifulness: what Scripture calls his *hesed* (loving-kindness), on which the covenant is built: that covenant rebuilt in the mercy of the incarnate Jesus.[9] In the end, the Jesus Prayer is not so much what we pray through the words but what the Spirit of the Lord prays through us: "In sighs too deep for words," as the Apostle also taught.

NOTES

1. In contemporary Roman Catholic practice, this is done by taking the right hand and putting the first two fingers together (a sign of the two natures of humanity and divinity united in Christ the Lord) and placing them on the forehead, stomach, left shoulder, and right shoulder (a cross signed over the whole body) while saying: "In the name of the Father, and of the Son, and of the Holy Spirit. Amen." In Orthodox practice (which was Western Catholic practice also until the seventeenth century), the sign of the cross is slightly different. The right hand is taken, and the first two fingers are placed together along with the thumb, as a sign of the Holy Trinity, and the three fingers are laid on the forehead, the stomach, the right shoulder, and the left shoulder, saying the same words as above.

2. A great collection of the writings of the saints on prayer is gathered together in the wonderful resource known as the *Philokalia*, published in several volumes by Faber & Faber from a team of translators including His Eminence Metropolitan Kallistos Ware. This is a great and lofty collection on prayer that will repay decades of study. A smaller collection of useful "prayer notes" taken directly from the ancient fathers and saints can be found in my own edition called *The Book of Mystical Chapters*, issued from Shambhala Press (2002).

3. The complete Psalms for Eastern Church's Great Compline are normally Pss. 4, 6, 12, 30, 34, and 90 LXX. For the Lesser Compline, the Psalms used are 50, 69, and 142 LXX.

4. A short passage from the Gospels may be read here. In Eastern ritual, it is usually a passage recounting the resurrection of Jesus, and designated an "Eothinon Gospel," since it connects the rising of the sun at the new dawn with the rising of the Christ.

5. These Three Psalms were added as a kind of coda, and so named to distinguish them from the "Six Psalms" of the beginning of Matins.

6. These verses are scriptural allusions based on the following: (RSV) Ps. 119:133; Ps. 119:22; Ps. 104:33.

7. *Syriac Slawoto.*

8. More about this can be found in my study titled *Standing in God's Holy Fire: The Byzantine Tradition* (Maryknoll, NY: Orbis, 2001).

9. More on this can be "seen" in the feature film appearing in 2011 entitled *Mysteries of the Jesus Prayer* (see www. mysteriesofthejesusprayer.com).

LIST OF ORIGINAL SOURCES

Agpia. Sydney: Coptic Orthodox Publications and Translations Board, 2000.

Mega Hieros Synekdemos. Athens: Phos, 1983.

Orologion to Mega. Athens: Asteros, 1973. (Greek Text)

The Liturgy of the Ethiopian Orthodox Tewahedo Church. Los Angeles: Feedel, 2000. (Ge'ez and Amhairic Text)

Theion Proseuchetarion. Athens: Endekate, 1988. (Greek Text)

About Paraclete Press

WHO WE ARE

Paraclete Press is a publisher of books, recordings, and DVDs on Christian spirituality. Our publishing represents a full expression of Christian belief and practice—from Catholic to Evangelical, from Protestant to Orthodox.

We are the publishing arm of the Community of Jesus, an ecumenical monastic community in the Benedictine tradition. As such, we are uniquely positioned in the marketplace without connection to a large corporation and with informal relationships to many branches and denominations of faith.

WHAT WE ARE DOING
Books

Paraclete publishes books that show the richness and depth of what it means to be Christian. Although Benedictine spirituality is at the heart of all that we do, we publish books that reflect the Christian experience across many cultures, time periods, and houses of worship. We publish books that nourish the vibrant life of the church and its people—books about spiritual practice, formation, history, ideas, and customs.

We have several different series, including the best-selling Paraclete Essentials and Paraclete Giants series of classic texts in contemporary English; A Voice from the Monastery—men and women monastics writing about living a spiritual life today; award-winning literary faith fiction and poetry; and the Active Prayer Series that brings creativity and liveliness to any life of prayer.

Recordings

From Gregorian chant to contemporary American choral works, our music recordings celebrate sacred choral music through the centuries. Paraclete distributes the recordings of the internationally acclaimed choir Gloriæ Dei Cantores, praised for their "rapt and fathomless spiritual intensity" by *American Record Guide,* and the Gloriæ Dei Cantores Schola, which specializes in the study and performance of Gregorian chant. Paraclete is also the exclusive North American distributor of the recordings of the Monastic Choir of St. Peter's Abbey in Solesmes, France, long considered to be a leading authority on Gregorian chant.

DVDs

Our DVDs offer spiritual help, healing, and biblical guidance for life issues: grief and loss, marriage, forgiveness, anger management, facing death, and spiritual formation.

Learn more about us at our website:
www.paracletepress.com, or call us toll-free at 1-800-451-5006.

ANCIENT SPIRITUAL DISCIPLINES

IN THIS NEW SERIES OF "LITTLE BOOKS" you will learn how to grasp the meaning of ancient ways of praying in a relatively short amount of time. This will leave you with the rest of your life to move beyond the reading and into the practicing!

PRAYING
with Icons

Linette Martin

64 pages
ISBN: 1-978-1-61261-058-0
$24.95 (pack of 5)
Small paperback

Icons point us beyond themselves. They are different from paintings. An icon speaks to both the mind and the soul. We respond in belief, or praise, or wonder, or encouragement, or simply—prayer.

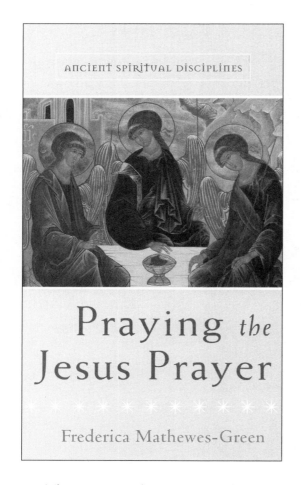

PRAYING
the Jesus
Prayer

Frederica
Mathewes-Green

64 pages
ISBN: 1-978-1-61261-059-7
$24.95 (pack of 5)
Small paperback

This very simple prayer was developed in the deserts of Egypt and Palestine during the early centuries of Christian faith and has been practiced in the Eastern Orthodox Church ever since. It is a prayer inspired by St. Paul's exhortation to "pray constantly" (1 Thessalonians 5:17), and its purpose is to tune one's inner attention to the presence of the Lord.

Available from most booksellers or
through Paraclete Press